MARSHWALKER

MANIT⬛BA

OAK HAMMOCK
WILDLIFE MANAGEMENT

MARSHWALKER
Naturalist Memoirs

by John Weier

with
illustrations by Rudolf Koes

 TURNSTONE PRESS

Turnstone Press
607 – 100 Arthur Street
Artspace Building
Winnipeg, Manitoba
R3B 1H3 Canada
www.TurnstonePress.com

Turnstone Press gratefully acknowledges the assistance of the
Canada Council for the Arts, the Manitoba Arts Council and
the Government of Canada through the Book Publishing
Industry Development Program for our publishing activities.

Le Conseil des Arts   The Canada Council
du Canada   for the Arts
depuis 1957   since 1957

ACKNOWLEDGEMENTS

One of these essays in slightly different form appeared in
Fresh Tracks: Writing the Western Landscape, Polestar Book Publishers.
The quote from *Things As They Are* by Guy Vanderhaeghe
is used by permission of McClelland & Stewart Inc. The quote
from *Desert Notes* by Barry Holstun Lopez is reprinted by
permission of Sterling Lord Literistic, Inc.
Thanks to David, and Daryl, and to the Manitoba Arts Council

Original cover photograph by Tom Thomson
Illustrations by Rudolf Koes
Design by Manuela Dias

This book was printed and bound in Canada by
Printcrafters, Inc. for Turnstone Press.

Canadian Cataloguing in Publication Data

Weier, John, 1949–

Marshwalker: naturalist memoirs

ISBN 0-88801-225-X

1. Oak Hammock Wildlife Management Area. 2. Marsh
ecology. 3. Weier, John, 1949–   I. Koes,
Rudolf.   II. Title.

QH87.3.W45 1998   577.68'097127'4   C98-920195-3

Especially,
for Susan

Table of Contents

Blue-winged teal pair

Long Silk Thread

*T*uesday, September 13. Suddenly the date seems important, something I should mark, a kind of holiday, a birthday. "September 13," I say it again out loud, take a deep breath like the pitchers do when they throw with a no-hitter into the ninth inning. Then I slam the back door to my house, painted green door, and listen for the lock to click. A piece of stucco rattles along the doorjamb, I push the thought aside, I'll try to fix that on Saturday. Today's the first day, my first day! I've got a fresh start, a new project, no time for home repairs! I hurry down the sidewalk, slide into the old car—Honda Civic—turn the key and poke my finger at the trip odometer, the engine whirs. I check the time. Nine a.m. I press my right foot against the gas pedal, my left pulls slowly off the clutch. The first day! I begin my drive to Oak Hammock Marsh.

I've imagined an experiment in writing and observation. These last years I've spent far too much time behind my desk, keyboard, computer; I've tired of my fiction and poetry, old manuscripts, old books, old words plucked from out of the stale air. Experiment, it sounds like dull science but it really isn't. The opposite. I want to see something new, write something new. I want my writing to hear, smell, feel. I want it to breathe! You can't say you live when you hunch every day in a soft chair, the same room, the only sensation where your bum meets the warm chair. Boredom. This experiment? I want to learn to write outside. Maybe I can discover something about the marsh. About birds. About weeds and mammals. About the world. I'd like to get lost for a while in the marsh, find myself lost at Oak Hammock Marsh.

I suppose this has been tried often enough by other people—Henry Thoreau on the Concord and Merrimack Rivers, Peter Matthiessen in the highlands of Nepal, pilgrims and travellers to Samarkand, to Tinker Creek, a thousand other seekers, would-be naturalists, I'm only muddling after them, there is nothing new. Still, what's the use of their experience to me? Should I just stay in my bed and read about it? No! What was Thoreau looking for? *I long ago lost a hound, a bay horse, and a turtledove, and am still on their trail;* my heart jumped when I first read his words twenty-five years ago. Last month I celebrated another birthday, turned forty-five years old, Thoreau's age when he died, I must be at least half done with this world. All those forty-five years I've waited for this one moment.

A small house, the one with the green door, where Susan and I live. Eight hundred square feet. Not the right house for us, I bought it six years ago before we even met, I'd been back single again for a while, I meant to stay that way. I hadn't lived in this house more than a month before I met Susan on a Sunday flight from Saskatoon to Winnipeg, some computer chip threw us together in the tail of the aircraft. She wore a black skirt and a brilliant checked wool blazer, pink and blue and gold. One empty seat between us, we talked and I dumped ginger ale on my leather jacket. By the end of our first coffee and dessert somehow we knew that we'd stay together, we felt suited. Not the right house, but we painted the outside, taupe, and hunter green, modern colours; we knocked out a wall and put in a new kitchen. I told Susan about my marsh idea. "Good," she said, she says that about all my ideas, most of them. But I'm not sure she understands, how could she? She wonders what I'll do out at the marsh for a whole day, she wonders about bugs and heat, Susan gets migraines from the sun and heat. I told her not to worry.

The nature of my exploration? I plan to visit Oak Hammock Marsh every month for a year or two, maybe three, to document what happens there in a day, from season to season, to look for changes, to weigh my reaction. I'll watch birds as they come and go, I'll carry a microcassette, put all these things on paper. I'll wander back through school with grass and trees and water, muskrats as classmates instead of humans. I hope one day to meet a red fox. Next week, between the creek and the Texas gate at the northwest corner, maybe I'll lunch with a coyote.

September 13. A quiet heavy morning, wind teases at the Esso flags along King Edward Street. Fog hangs and drifts through parts of the city. Earlier today I couldn't see the tops of downtown forty-storey office towers from Ellice Avenue, the city suddenly grown flat for a few hours, and fifty years younger. The temperature this morning is six degrees Celsius. Cold. Autumn. The forecast on the TV weather channel when I ate my breakfast promised twenty-two degrees, sun and cloud. I drive from my home through industrial Winnipeg north along Highway 7. The clouds ahead of me float high and light. After the last big warehouse at the edge of town, farms, a grain field on the left—hillocks of swath—a fence, pasture with a mixed herd of cattle on the right, barns and sheds, stacks of hay and straw. I remember another morning on this same drive, early—where was I going? off to visit a banjo player near Warren?—when a fox frolicked in the snow and the stubble. This close to city the horizon still clutters with hydro: poles, power lines and insulators, strutting metal erectors. And then the fog again.

To the northeast a farmyard blurs through the mist, trees hover almost into focus as I approach, then they're gone. Nothing but fog beyond the first half mile all around me.

I see starlings flying in formation, mourning doves on the wire, crows on fence posts, rock doves, a great blue heron flapping low over a field of clover, one cormorant winging north against the highway. Off to my right, on a side road, a ring-billed gull stalks an easy meal. Two western meadowlarks play above the wild oats and thistle. Beyond the meadowlarks, a thick scarlet carpet in the ditch, so striking. Is it a grass? A flower? I stop the car on the shoulder and walk. Four, eight inches tall; such a swollen red stem, triangular leaf, looks and feels like a succulent. I turn pages, *Wildflowers Across the Prairies*, so many colourful species in my wildflower book. Good thing about plants, they don't fly away while you try to identify them. There. Red samphire: a ground-cover plant found in bogs and marshes of the southern prairies, turns red when it matures. I wonder how many times I've driven past that plant and not noticed it.

The fog grows heavier. It fits the morning, a kind of symbol for the start of my experiment. What can I possibly find at Oak Hammock? And how will I ever write about it? What do I know about birds and marshes and plants? Not much! I'm no scientist, biologist. No naturalist, a bird-watcher of a few years, nothing more. On quiet days sometimes I hear house finches twittering at the edge of my imagination. Two, three years; I feel staggered by the size of what I've begun. All I do know is that one small memory, a childhood dream, something to do with forest and creeks and nature, tracking and birchbark canoes, the outdoors, wolves, the call of the wild. I had a wish once to be a forest ranger.

The fog breaks and lifts, then settles in again as I pass the penitentiary at Stony Mountain. I think of those men, several hundred of them, boxed and barred inside their grey stone buildings. What a tired life. I joined them there with my guitar in 1981, folk festival band, watched them from the stage, drank coffee at the same table, I hated the clank and all the metal bars. What percentage of them are Native? High, I've heard. Forest and birchbark, outdoors, I wonder how they will ever find their way again. The sky above me turns suddenly blue, but on the ground fog, thicker and thicker. I turn east on Highway 67, catch a halo and the sun deep inside a cloud. More pastures, barns, fences, and a willow on the left slipping from green to yellow brown. Then a barn swallow, two, three, their busy dip and roll and dive, back and forth, up and down, loops and corners. I do know barn swallows, their chatter and their long forked tails, their mud nests, had them on the farm where I grew up. Can birds be happy? Do we know about that? Dogs sure can, their tails. I always imagined that swallows must be happy, the way they fly, a statement about their psychology. *A happy and active young bird . . .*

Oak Hammock Marsh, thirty minutes, thirty-nine kilometres from home. I slow and turn north on the gravel road into the marsh, I pull the car off to the side. A swarm of blackbirds greets me. Spotted, speckled, striped blackbirds, red-winged, probably immature many of them, you can see the patches beginning to show on some of their wings. Blackbird swirl. More barn swallows too, and a sparrow sulking in the underbrush. What's that? In the distance, the sound of guns, hunters' guns. So how many species have I seen? Red-winged blackbird, one. Two is the barn swallow. I'll start counting here at the gravel road. Off behind that row of trees I hear a goldfinch, there, yellow, and its stuttering flight.

The hunters' guns, I feel a wrenching in my gut; guns, something I hadn't expected this first morning in the marsh. Duck hunting season? Goose? I'm not sure which it is. Three, an American goldfinch. That sparrow I noticed in the brush, what was it? A song sparrow? A white-throated? I touched my first gun when I was still a child, at home on the fruit farm, a shotgun my father borrowed to shoot grackles out of the cherry trees. He only used it once, said the gun did more damage to the cherry crop than the grackles had. And I've held very few guns since, still too much the Mennonite, only fired three or four shots, at a tin can in St. Ambrose when a friend of mine insisted. The crash of guns again, grown men still playing at death.

Two mallards fluff and preen their feathers among the grasses of the first Oak Hammock Marsh ditch. Ducks have an oil gland at the base of the tail, they rub their bill on it, then clean and smooth all their feathers. Four, I suppose, is the mallard. Five, the white rump and rust-brown breast of a northern harrier, marsh hawk, it weaves and bobs as it hunts along the side of the road. A flock of ring-billed gulls, heads tucked, rests on the summer fallow. That's six. Western meadowlark sings in the distance. Seven. Counting bird species, birdwatcher habits, I don't know what else to do out here at the marsh. And still the sound of guns. These guns could be farm equipment though—cannons, *Kanonen*, my father used to call them at home on the fruit farm— scatter guns set to scare the migrating geese off the fields of grain. Some farmers in Niagara used to set them in their orchards.

A savannah sparrow hops from branch to branch in a low clump of willow twenty metres east of the car. Behind it, hundreds of blackbirds again, black specks churning in the morning sky. I can't tell what they are, too far away; probably red-wings, Brewer's, cowbirds, a mixture, you see that in the fall. Nesting boxes, they look like bluebird houses, hang from the sides of hydro poles. I've never seen bluebirds here at the marsh but tree swallows use these boxes in spring and summer, chatter in long rows on the wires. Now, the tree swallows are gone, before their barn cousins. Three, four geese fly over the marsh interpretive centre to the north. One goose low over the first pond. Nine species, that Canada goose. There, two more geese. Eight, ten, twelve geese to the west. I wonder about the snowy owl. I saw a snowy owl crouched there on that mound of earth several weeks ago. Will I see it today? Where has it gone?

We've been to Oak Hammock before, Susan and I, many times, we started following birds soon after we met. I'd already bought binoculars and a Peterson bird book; Susan had watched her grandfather, he chased birds too, she didn't think it too strange. We drove out south of Portage la Prairie to hike one Sunday, found a great horned owl in a farmyard, took a long hour to name it. Those first bird excursions thrilled and tired us. Each new bird, in the book, on the tree, in the book again, until our eyes ached. Comparing our observations, colours and features, "Susan, what do you see?" Winnipeg. Qu'Appelle. Jasper. Squamish. Tofino. We couldn't name half the birds we saw. We noticed though that other birdwatchers counted, kept lists, so many species, so many robins, crows; we learned a few tricks from them.

One northern shoveller shovels for seed round the edge of the pond just south of the interpretive buildings. A killdeer calls in the parking lot, runs, and stops, and calls. A robin sings in the willow bluff behind me. I park the car, get out, gather my lunch and knapsack. Suddenly, an unfamiliar call, sounds almost like a chuckle, a goose I think, but not a Canada. Only one goose in that direction, circling over the shoveller pond, waiting to land, webbed feet spread, wings pushing down the air. I sprint ten metres to get a better look, fumble with my binoculars. A short neck. Orange feet and legs. Patch of white around the bill. Greater white-fronted goose, must have flown in with a flock of Canada geese. Laughter tickles my lungs, that's a species I haven't seen too often, and the first time I noticed its call.

The grass sparkles with dew, wet shoes. I walk back to the car to lock it. Geese all around. Groups of two, four, eight, fourteen, sixteen, flying in every direction. I step from the parking lot onto the boardwalk and into the Oak Hammock willow bluff. A bit of movement on a branch. White eye-ring, white wing bars, a ruby-crowned kinglet, such a tiny bird, though I don't see its crown. More kinglets, and a fall yellow-rumped warbler, the willows full of

passerines. I walk farther. A Swainson's thrush trills in the
north. He sounds weak, congested, not at all the clarity of
his song last spring. Female yellow warbler perches close
beside me, female or immature. Speckled blur, a downy
woodpecker settles in a dead tree, rattles up and down the
trunk. A few more steps. American tree sparrows gather low
along the water, a white-throated sparrow *chinks* to its com-
panions, more yellow-rumps flicker by. This marsh, and
morning, my head spins with wonder. Where did these
birds come from? Where will they go? What appetites carry
them? That American redstart—sometimes called fire-tail,
or *Candelita* in Latin America, "little torch"—that redstart,
sparkling black and orange and white, its fanned tail, how
far has it flown since yesterday?

The sunlight rests so calm, and the blue sky, the willows
almost moving, just a hint of wind at their leaf-tips, the
smell of burning stubble. I kneel as another redstart flutters
by, immature this time. Here, under the boardwalk, the
water a blanket of spotted green, thousands of pinprick
leaves over a three-metre circle. What is it, some kind of
algae? The book says lesser duckweed, each tiny leaf has its
own root on the underside.

An explosion of sound. Loud honking, the whistle and
fart of wings. A hundred Canada geese fly just metres above
my head, remarkable how much noise those wings make
when you hear them this close. There, a blackpoll warbler,
very orange legs. My body slowly begins to unwind, muscles
loosen, here in the open, away from the study, the sun warm
against my skin. Pleasure! I sink back to lean against a railing, close my eyes. And then another alarm! I start up. A
squawk, a patch of chalky blue, six blue-winged teal break
from the water beside me. A common snipe coughs, flies
round in front of me. Snipe with their short legs and long
bill, their grassy habits, if not secretive, certainly not as easily seen as other sandpipers. Another snipe, five or six of
them. A rustle, a rusty wing, a swamp sparrow flutters in the
dried reeds just a foot above the marsh. The air fills with

birds and calls. The sun brightens. The wind wakes. Willows and grass, cattails begin to wave. Off to my right, below the wood-duck box, the careful white and black striped crown, grey collar, pink bill of the white-crowned sparrow. The slate-black hood of the dark-eyed junco, just three metres more. Another sudden burst, wings, too small for a robin, a dark bird flashes by. What was it?

That dark-eyed junco, he's twenty-six, I've kept a list.

Many years ago my father told me about his experiences hunting. That was in the '30s, long before I was born, south and west of here, near Killarney—he'd walk out on the prairie with his gun, watch for jackrabbits. The Dirty Thirties. Money was scarce, food expensive, you could half feed a family by hunting. Even so, my father's hunting life didn't last long, he couldn't bear to watch those long-limbed rabbits die. He told me that sometimes when he shot them they cried like a baby; he had babies at home, my older brother and sister, he didn't like to watch those rabbits struggle and die.

I leave the boardwalk and the trees and walk east past the observation mound and deeper into the marsh. Here, away from the shelter of the bluff, the air feels a bit colder, I pull my jacket close. I see a pied-billed grebe, black circle on its bill, it dives. A second great blue heron. An American bittern, I think, *uuonk-a-lunk, uuonk-a-lunk, uuonk-a-lunk,* no wonder they call it the slough pump. Yes; up and down along the grasses and gone before I even find my binoculars. A double-crested cormorant flies north along the water. A greater yellowlegs calls, *tu tu tu,* its informal address. Another yellowlegs stands on the shore, one leg up, beak in, and out, under the wing, resting. A lesser yellowlegs stalks by. Probably a scaup there, a greater scaup—that's thirty-three species—turns, arches its neck and curves into the water. A Brewer's blackbird zigs through the cut grass.

The marsh has stayed lush and green this year even into September. We've had so much rain, far more than usual, and spread throughout the summer. Even in Winnipeg, the lawns far brighter than last year, and the noise of lawn-mowers. Now, a warm fall. No frost yet this year. Vegetable gardens still red with tomatoes, leaves still cling to the trees. Lots of ducks in the marsh in September: blue-winged teal, mallards, scaups, redheads, ducks sometimes so hard to name in fall. In spring these same species trumpet their identity, shout it to their mates. There, a lesser scaup with its peaked head, the white spot on its face, the only fall identifiers. White bill, grey body, an American coot; that one bird you can't ever confuse. Another rasping cough, a chorus of three common snipe flies from the mud shore.

That greater yellowlegs at the turn of the first trail seems tireless, its search unending. It steps back and forth in the shallow water. Steps deeper. Darts to the right, turns. Rushes to the left. Stretches its neck, bill into the water. Out again. In. Out. What's it looking for? A shriek! The yellowlegs start, four of them. A merlin bursts by, hunting. The yellowlegs remain, and a smaller sandpiper feeding now along the mud flat. Short legs, scalloped back and wings. Too big for a least sandpiper, legs and wings too short for a white-rumped, I'm not sure what it is.

How do you describe the call of a snow goose? The conventional goose *honk* doesn't quite seem to handle it. *Aaaeeiiih.* Is it a scream? Two hundred shadows slide past my feet. Maybe three hundred, snow geese, white phase and blue, flying south. Wheeling. Flying north. East, then south again. High above. I walk farther and farther into the marsh. I watch another kinglet, ruby-crowned, flirting in the marsh grass. I hear a goldfinch. And then a savannah sparrow. A muskrat vees through the water. The snow geese are coming west again. Far above them a single-engine plane drones by. Slough grasses, cattails whisper and wave in the breeze, settle again as the wind dies, whisper and settle. Water hemlock—common across the prairies—beside the trail, its long serrated leaves, deadly poison, you see it on the poison chart in your doctor's office. Still no marsh wrens today, a month ago I would have heard their chatter everywhere.

Northern pintail

A white heron, suddenly it's there. Black legs, a yellow bill, great egret. Something like a ghost, not a wing flap, no sound; the egret floats by and drops into the grasses far behind me. Then it's up again, an aerobatic meditation, back and forth, back and forth in front of me, pressing the slow air with its wing. I love to watch these egrets, each sighting for me a celebration, a spectacle not that common for me here in Manitoba. A flock of blackbirds joins the display, flies behind the egret, the white wing-patch of the yellow-headed blackbird shining in the light.

Egrets. Just last year, on a drive to Texas, Susan and I climbed a fence and stumbled across a farmer's pasture. We felt guilty, we were trespassing, and we were also afraid of the bull; the pasture was home to a large herd of cattle, I had to do some convincing to get Susan to join me. We set our

11

tripod and scope on a rusty piece of farm machinery, Caterpillar, marooned in the middle of the field. We were looking for one snowy egret we thought we'd spotted from the road as we drove, found instead a heronry. Hundreds of them—great egrets, snowy egrets, cattle egrets, great blue herons, black-crowned night herons—perched in trees, in brush, on nests, or flying. A breeding colony, lost in a hollow in the middle of some old farm, by some stroke of luck or miracle. Herons, more in one place than we'd seen in all our birding combined, I think it was in Oklahoma, home of the scissor-tailed flycatcher and the redbud tree.

I've walked some distance now, the Oak Hammock Centre lies far behind me. The birds have become more wary. And so have I. I tiptoe from one stand of whitetop to another. Two chocolate redheads lurk in the slough grass. A pied-billed grebe, alarmed at seeing me, forgets to dive as it might have, raises and flaps its short wings, legs almost falling behind, patting, running along the water, finds a clump of mud and reeds to hide behind. A cormorant spatters across the lake, wings tipping the water on each black stroke away from me. The water ripples, a fish maybe, I have seen minnows in this marsh. Dragonflies shimmer and rattle in the sun; they pair and mate, even here on the late summer trail around me.

Small yellow moths, white moths, dark brown moths with orange markings hover in the air. I hear the guts and rolling *u-u-urck, a-u-u-urck* of a raven. Then a stretch of silence. *Cro-unnk, cro-unnk, cro-unnk,* I look up, fifteen sandhill cranes laze high in the sky, necks down and stretched, legs dragging behind them. A flock of gulls just below them, the still-almost-black head of a Franklin's, the black wing-edge of the Bonaparte's gull. I just can't think what else to say, how else to respond, but surprise! Herons, dragonflies, moths, warblers, ducks, sparrows, kinglets, blackbirds. The shock of so much life here in the marsh, in this wilderness, just before the frost. So much activity, I can hardly think about myself, about men, women, the city. All this life living on here without us.

Wilderness? Is this marsh a wilderness? I'm glad to get away from people, away from plans and civilization. I'm glad to be alone, isolate, joined with the birds and the brush and the cattails. Where was Barry Lopez when he wrote his *Desert Notes*? How many miles was he from the nearest human thing? What was it Ernest Thompson Seton found in 1882 in Manitoba? Maybe this is the only wilderness I have left, the only wilderness a city man can manage, if I crouch down low enough I can't see any buildings. A wilderness close to home, I can drive here anytime, any day, week. I can stop here on my way to do the shopping. I'm always home for night.

People talk about silence, about the quiet of God, the call of a spirit, when they talk about wilderness—I like the sound of that. The Russian philosopher Ouspensky, sipping his vodka, what did he mean: *the silence of a forest or a prison*. There is silence here. Of a kind. Silence for me, human silence. Except when I'm talking, into my new Olympus microcassette. No radio, no television. Now I hear a different sound. I hear the flush of a sparrow in the grass, the rustle of the wind passing. I hear the call of the Canada geese, the *krish krish* of insects along the water. I hear the sound of seeds popping, the sun is getting hot.

I hear a yellowlegs, the whistle of the mallard wings. I hear the blue-winged teal, *aaawwwkk*, hear the depth of its fear—it didn't see me till I was far too close. I hear the sound of a fly buzzing in my ear. I hear footsteps. I hear the sound of my two feet, walking. Finally, after almost three hours in the marsh, I hear the warble—white eye-stripe and brown crown—the chatter of a marsh wren. I'm writing the story of one man, alone, in the wilderness. One man, myself, almost alone, I see a tractor two fields over. A kind of man, if you wonder; I do cry at movies, and at Christmas, I don't think women come from Venus. This marsh, almost a wilderness. I look behind me. Someone is following.

They say that baby spiders leave their nests by wafting on the breeze at the end of long silk threads, parachute threads; they say they can travel that way for hundreds of kilometres. I believe that. Silk threads have gathered all around me on my walk, spider silk, they cling to me. First this morning's fog, and now these cobwebs. I'm caught in the middle of a cobweb. Almost like a bride, draped in cobwebs, trailing white behind me, and the sun sparkling on each line. Out here in the middle of the marsh, I must be celebrating something, I wonder what it is, wonder whether anybody knows. It's almost one o'clock. The sun feels hot on my back. I haven't prepared for the heat today. Now, the sun baking down, I take my white hanky, knot it at the corners, pull it over my head the way my mother taught me at home in the orchard; I've reached the age where my scalp needs protection. The birds seem to have noticed the heat too, they've hidden from the burning light, just one pied-billed grebe here beside me. But what are grebes afraid of? If the sun gets too hot, they need only dive, take their pied bills below the surface of the water to cool.

A bend in the trail and the ground drops suddenly in front of me, edge of the earth. I am blind to the shape of the Oak Hammock Centre in the west, to the bales and fields of the farmer in the east, houses in the south. The marsh spins out into one big lake, into shores and islands. I see a single bench, a trail sign, a hill; nothing else. The morning fog and clouds are gone; the sky is deep, and very very blue. I settle on the bench at the top of the hill, pull crackers and dried fruit and juice from my knapsack, a muffin that Susan baked. Without any sound or warning, a mile from any tree, ten pine siskins descend on a patch of thistle beside me. I think suddenly of my list; pine siskin, that's a total of forty-seven species.

The siskins flutter and *chir-r-r* as only pine siskins can, they peck at the seed of the thistle, a few moments, then they're gone, high in the air. I finish my snack, reach down for my sack; on the ground at my feet, little paw prints, handprints in the mud. Whose are they? Where do they go? I imagine a humped back, a simple black mask. I get up and I walk. I will answer these prints. Let's see where their trail takes me. Handprints in the mud, is this a racoon I'm following?

Snow geese

Goose Gabble

*E*ven as I left home this morning I thought about guns. I'm upset about hunting, not at all what I wanted from my marsh visits, to see dead geese, hear the crackle of guns. The hunters, they'll be out for sure today, this is the middle of their season. I read in a waterfowl magazine last week that the Canadian Air Force dropped half a million bombs on Oak Hammock Marsh during World War II, target practice. Birds, mammals, plants; can you imagine what all they killed? When I told Susan about this she wondered whether bombs might still be leaking old poison into marsh water, whether there were any bombs left unexploded, we wondered how safe I'd be on my trail. "Do be careful," she said. I've read stories about the hunt that John James Audubon attended near New Orleans on the 16th of March, 1821. Audubon estimated that forty-eight thousand golden plovers were slaughtered by market gunners in the hunting frenzy of that one day. Guns! Hunters!

Wednesday, September 28. Three degrees this morning in Winnipeg. Cloudy, though the clouds are high. A west wind, light. The forecast predicts a high of seventeen, sun, no rain. I've dropped Susan off at work, she finished her lipstick in the car; by 7:45 I'm on the road to the marsh again. I ate my usual breakfast before we left the house, an orange, yogurt, cereal. Still, I stop at McDonald's to pick up an Egg McMuffin and coffee. I remember how hungry I got at Oak Hammock two weeks ago, the lunch I packed far too small, fresh air and appetite. After McDonald's I drive north. Past patches of stubble. And one crop standing, a field of wheat on the left side of Highway 8 just outside the Winnipeg Perimeter. September 28, that's late for wheat, probably because of the rain this year. Maybe this field flooded in spring and had to be seeded again, maybe it's just been too wet for the swather and the combine.

I've started thinking about frost, the first fall frost, I'm sure I have a memory of August frost, but nothing this year yet. Trees, however, are starting to show a lot of reds and yellows. Most of the hardwoods sheltering this farmyard on my left have kept their leaves, just a few trunks stretch naked against the horizon, maybe they're dead ones. And that long line of poplars along the driveway to the right— thirty, forty poplars—all of them still green, but one tree, exactly ten from the road, has turned colour. One tree, and one different drummer.

Morning. I wish Susan were in the car, I wish it were five a.m. and we were on our way somewhere, Susan and I have taken a lot of touring trips together, combination bird trips usually. Vancouver Island. The Gaspé. Niagara. Corpus Christi. The way we smile at each other the first morning on the road, the excited way our hands grip, the first egg breakfast stop after three hours' driving. I used to make all my trips in a rush, load the car and drive for twenty hours, nibble from a bag of lunch. Hurry to get there, hurry home, vacations that left you feeling empty. Susan has slowed me down, taught me to stop for meals, pull into a motel early, bring a book to read evenings. Other trips too, by air: San Francisco, New Delhi, Chicago. We've planned them far in advance, shaped a full year around them.

As I approach the marsh entrance the sky fills with geese. Snow geese, white phase and their black primaries, the blues with white heads; and Canada geese, a white chin strap. Many more geese than last time, clouds of them, all thinking south. Change and time. In the last two weeks, I guess, the geese have taken notice. The sky swarms with chevrons and clusters and single straggling lines.

I've set my first task today to collect leaves from the two bunches of trees here at the Oak Hammock gravel entrance, I'd like to know what kind of trees they are. I can recognize wood once it's cut and machined—oak, mahogany, Hawaiian koa, big-leaf maple, spruce—I learned that working with guitars and violins, the craft of lutherie, but I know nothing about the trees. I park the car, step across the road, and search my way through the ditch. Looks pretty muddy. My ears ring with the clamour of geese and blackbirds. A flock of Canadas vees overhead, one snow goose among them. I catch a flash of red in the poplars, red-winged blackbird. Two rock doves strut on the old hip-roof barn. The barn swallows seem to have flown since my last visit.

When Jonathan was four he got crazy about guns; must have learned it from the television. Or was it in his genes? We didn't buy him any, his mother and I—that was twelve years ago, long before Susan—didn't think children should learn to play with weapons. Guns aren't for playing, we said. So he made them, built them out of Lego. A hundred guns, cartons full of guns, a bedroom full of guns. He knew their names—rifle, machine gun—he knew their purpose. Guns are for killing. What a battle we had. Old against young, weak against strong, we weren't the strong ones. What could we say? You're not allowed to build guns out of Lego? He would have made them out of milk jugs, or newspaper. *Ttsshwww, ttsshwww.* He would have used his mouth and his fingers, he had to have a gun.

I break clusters of leaves from this first stand of trees, I mean to take them home, dry and press them. A stem with three yellow leaves, I study their shapes, I've brought a book. Box elder, Manitoba maple, the book says that box elder grows along river and stream banks, beside roads, in wild places. The other is a bush, still green, some kind of caragana, I think. I stalk the second clump of trees. The grass clumsy with dew, my shoes and pant legs grow heavy, wet. I pick more leaves. These are oval, egg-shaped, and turning brown, not poplar at all like I'd thought from the road, probably elm. I should have known, I grew up with two huge poplars at the end of our farm drive. One summer day when I was six or seven, while we were running from the tomato patch, crash, a bolt of lightning tore the bark off one of those poplars. I turn with my collection of leaves and a common snipe scares up along the ditch at my feet; a flash of rusty tail, the zigzag flight, rustle of leaves and wind its only sound.

Now I hear guns, a rush of them, these are the hunters.

Back in the car I turn the heater on my legs and watch as twenty Brewer's blackbirds perch in the Manitoba maple. A male with his black and purple sheen, yellow eye. The female, brown, brown eye, and dull. They *check* and wheeze, jump from branch to branch. A few short years ago I'd never heard of Brewer's blackbirds, then Susan and I identified a pair on a back road in British Columbia, binoculars and book; our first year birding, Squamish, Susan had a job there when we met. A dozen red-wings fly in to join the Brewer's, sit for a while, then fly off again. I hear the *tseep* of a sparrow. I see a flash of white on a hunting hawk, a northern harrier. He flaps. Glides. Flaps. Twists and turns. Flaps again, plummets to the stubble. He's up again, flying, three, six metres above the ground. He turns his head into the sky, dives, this time he stays down, feeding, he's caught something.

The first creek here at the marsh entrance doesn't offer one duck today. North and west of that, though, the stubble is spotted with geese, snows and Canadas. I notice the young of the snow geese, they're not fully grown, and they're grey, they haven't taken mature colours yet. I stop and watch for a while, listen. Geese, heads up, heads down. Waddling, left and right. Stretching their wings, resting. All their goose gabble. I almost feel they're talking to me, about me. I wish I could tell you something about the sound of five thousand geese calling, the way that sound touches me, the quiet it brings inside me. And then I hear the guns again. The hunters are close now, I've seen them crouched in the fields. Their trucks and Broncos park on shoulders and mounds. My whispered warning to the geese, I know, completely useless.

I drive farther. There! A yellow bill and eye, red spot on the mandible, pink legs, black wing-tips and grey mantle. A herring gull stands alone on the summer fallow, big gull. Who's that behind the gull? Some smaller birds fluffing their feathers far behind the herring. I can't make out what they are, even with my twenty-two-power telescope. Oh, here we go, they're up. Shorebirds, fifty or a hundred of them. They bend and curl, I see their white bellies, dark backs, white, dark, white, back and forth, all in a sequence. They dip behind a bluff of trees. Gone.

The car rolls into a stall in front of the interpretive centre. Six ducks rest on this first pond. Five show the sloping beak and forehead of the canvasback, favourite of North American hunters and epicures, the other is a dark eyed American wigeon. Six ducks drift on the water, one preens the feathers behind her neck, the other ruffles her wing, shakes her head and beak. They turn this way and that on the pond. Four mallards fly up in alarm, mallards often seem to be the first of the ducks to fly. I hear the twitter of American tree sparrows, dark-eyed juncos, Harris' and white-crowned sparrows in the shrubs and thistle.

How will I get used to this, to being here? So much to see here at the marsh, so much I want to see, to learn. I feel almost blinded by the marsh. I can't find anything to think about, write about, there's too much to write about. My thoughts clutter with detail. The chaos of the marsh. Each individual marking of a ruby-crowned kinglet, a robin, yellow-rumped warbler; white eye-ring, white wing bar, white lower belly, white throat, yellow crown patch. The variety of weeds and trees and bushes, greens and greys and browns. They say you only see the things you can name, that's one way to calm this chaos. Not much has changed along the boardwalk, the passerines still here, active in the willows, maybe a few less. A common snipe, the blue-winged teal. And yet everything seems far busier than last time.

A pair of rusty blackbirds. I see the rust-brown of his back, brown stripes above and below his eye, black lower back and tail, the buff breast of the female. This bird stockier than the Brewer's I saw earlier, the first good look I've ever had at a rusty blackbird. A song sparrow with its black moustache, the yellow eyebrow of a savannah sparrow. Maybe the willows have changed; there are fewer warblers— maybe the warblers are almost gone—more sparrows, and these rusty blackbirds.

I pull more clothing out of my knapsack. Two shirts, two sweaters, a cap, wool socks, I'm glad I brought extra so I could dress warmer today.

An American pipit pumps its black tail on a dried branch three metres in front of me, I see the white outer tail feathers. The pipit, another sparrow-sized and sparrow-streaked bird to frustrate the beginning birder, as though twenty species of sparrow weren't already enough. Even a western meadowlark singing still in the willow bluff. And those secretive swamp sparrows, they fly up, just up, a foot above the marsh, they rustle through the brush, and then they're down again. Somehow, you never get a real look at them. Beyond the willows, lesser yellowlegs traverse the grass. I hear a greater yellowlegs, there, he flies from the water's edge, stutters along the reeds. Two snipe *harsh* out of the slough grass. I see a coot, a lesser scaup. Has anything else changed in two weeks? The air is cool.

I feel like a wild man, early *Homo sapiens*, *Homo erectus*, like Adam wakened in his teeming Eden. I'm so anxious to see, I start to run. I run past the pied-billed grebe, past the rustling cane grass, white plume and scarlet stalk, past another grebe, past trail sign and fork. What did I think, if I could name everything perfectly, I would fall back into the Garden? Out of breath, I slow to a walk again. And walk. And walk. The same path as last time, but faster. I hope to get far out into the marsh today, I've reached the open water already. The geese to the south of me fly up. They watch, and wait. Fly up, and wait again. Here's a dragonfly, one small dragonfly alone. Even the dragonfly seems to have lost its colour now, a pale and rusted brown. To the north, that could be the double-crested cormorant that tipped the water for me last time. It's still sitting on the same mound of mud and reeds. The cormorant starts, jerks around. Is it the wind? The season? Is it me? There's a panic in the air today. I feel it. Is mine the same one the ducks and geese feel? Are they as anxious to move as I am? I need to find a place to sit, to shift my thoughts to one small duck. I'll wait for this marsh to come to me. I need to stop running. I can say *this* for the hunters, they're far more patient than I. Still, I walk faster, I hear my breath begin to blow.

This trail is far shorter than I thought. Just to my right I see the mound and the bench where I lunched last time, I told Susan about it, we had never walked that far. And one great blue heron still left at the marsh. Crook-necked, long wings lined with black, black stripe above the eye, it swings over the mound into the east, passes low in front of me. The wings stop, the heron slips by, flaps again, braces itself to land. Two kilometres from the parking lot and boardwalk, I carry a map. Today I'll walk a big loop around this marsh, seven more kilometres before I'm back at the car. I hike up along the creek on the eastern boundary of the Oak Hammock property. The great blue, in the creek, there it is again, long legs straddled, yellow bill fixed straight into the west. And beside me, finally, my first horned grebes of the year; white cheeks and throat, dark crown and nape, their winter colours. The grebes rush to hide among the drying cattails.

I march on.

An injured mallard flops across the trail in front of me, flops into the tall grass. Maybe gun shot. Food for a coyote or a fox, I guess, for an eagle later in the season. Those human hunters, I wonder what they're looking for, their idea may not be that different from mine. Get out of the office, away from the job, find a patch of sun to lie in. My great blue heron again, can't get any rest today, must wonder what I'm chasing. It's up so close and flies right at me, for a moment I think it's going to hit me. So close I can see the detail on the chestnut at the front edge of the wing, I hadn't ever noticed all that colour before.

Sparrows flutter all along this trail, but I have left them to their own designs. Sparrows can be so difficult, especially in fall; are much easier to identify in spring, by their colour or their song. Are these savannahs? Are they Le Conte's, grasshoppers? Could they be sharp-tailed sparrows? Adult, or immature? Their sparrow coats appear pale and ragged. Last September, in Halifax, Susan and I hired a guide for fifty dollars to find a sharp-tailed sparrow for us. We drove north of the city with him, visited all the good birding spots, saw numerous new species. Late in the afternoon we parked beside a strip of marsh and sand for our sharp-tailed. That poor sparrow was determined not to give us a look, our guide just as eager to put the seal on his day's earnings. Susan and I waited, binoculars in hand, while he bustled about the marsh flushing sparrows. "No, no. There, it flew over there." We seemed always to be looking in the wrong direction, our guide was getting angry. I hear a rustle in the slough grass. I step closer. A muskrat splashes into the water. So what am I doing here? Just like the Halifax guide, frightening the ducks, robbing the great blue heron of a quiet morning, giving that group of hunters something more substantial than a goose to shoot at.

A ground squirrel, striped and spotted back, stirs in the

grass, waits by its hole. When I'm two feet away, suddenly it's gone, it too is wary of me. Thirteen-lined ground squirrel, a bold pattern, seven dark and six paler stripes; yesterday I would have been satisfied with "prairie dog." Maybe this is the nature of my wilderness, that I am a stranger in the marsh, that creatures are wary of me. Farther to the east, finally, a flock of ring-billed gulls inspects the mud flats; our common gull, I had expected to see them much sooner. My second trail sign, with a line map and distances, I turn west, six kilometres to go. The wind rushes in my ears. A hundred paces down the trail I see a flash of white on the north water, something new, a duck I haven't seen since early summer. The white neck and breast, long pointed black tail feathers, erect bearing of a northen pintail.

What does Barry Lopez say? *The desert is like a boulder; you expect to wait. You expect night to come. Morning. Winter to set in. But you expect sometime it will loosen into pieces to be examined. When it doesn't, you weary.* I imagine Lopez might say the same thing about the marsh, that the marsh will never give you what you expect. Here in this marsh all the usual rules are gone, you can only wait. When you think you've finally waited long enough, you'll still have to wait a little longer.

Now I wish I had my telescope. Of course, it's in the car, four, five kilometres away. Off to the south dark duck-shapes balance in the water. And two bigger daubs of white. Tails high in the air, necks, I suppose, stretched to the muddy bottom. Must be tundra swans. What was it I read about swans, how they and ducks benefit each other? Swans stir food from the bottom of a pond while the ducks feed on the surface. The ducks act as sentinels, watch for predators, warn the swans by flying. Tundra swans, I can see the line of their necks, their black beaks. I turn and step from the swans. A ring-necked duck scuttles away, black back, striped bill; I see the trace and curve of his pale sides. A coot gallops across the lake after him.

This bench. I have added and subtracted the kilometres,

this is the farthest I'll be from the parking lot today. The centre of the marsh, I can hide here for a while. I'm finally alone. The horizon reaches for miles and miles. In the east the clouds fluff and roll. In the south, if I squint, the glimmer of the city, skyscrapers. To the west, one dark cloud and a line of trees. North, haze of a farmer's tractor in the distance. The sky is overcast. The grass and earth sponge under my feet. Common groundsel, wild alfalfa, dandelion still blooming, thistle, goose droppings and feathers, a touch of brown earth. I'll sit and wait on this bench, see what the world brings to me.

Water pushes all around this trail. Among the rushes and the reeds at the back of the pond in front of me stands a wooden cross, one black cormorant spreads and dries its water-soaked wings on either arm. Cormorants, I've discovered, need to dry their wings after diving to feed, their feathers aren't waterproofed the way that ducks' are, not to the same extent. The pond swarms with waterfowl: mallards, American coots, another pintail, a few scaups, one common goldeneye. Yellowlegs *tu tu* up and down the strand. A northern shoveller bows, down and up, with her wide spoon bill. Down, up, down. Down, up. She gives her head a shake. Down again, only her tail end visible, orange legs still paddling. Behind her a group of ruddy ducks, three or four—so this is where the ruddy ducks live in September—dark cap, pale cheek, tail still cocked, the male has lost his ruddy colour.

Not much happens around my bench in the marsh in one hour. Just the rustling of the grass and the wind. Just a hundred ducks resting and feeding. Just a cormorant stretching its wings against a cross, a ruddy duck with an upright tail, a blue-winged teal flashing by. Just my head, wondering what it should be thinking.

That ruddy duck male dives closer. I think for a moment how lucky I am this is September and not June. The mosquitoes, I don't know what I'll do next June. I think of the ducks, that shoveller feeding. Does that shoveller think about mosquitoes? Do mosquitoes bite her? And does she think about me? She knows I'm here. She watches. She swims away as I walk closer. She must think I'm dangerous. How did she learn that? If I sit quiet on a bench, I wonder if they'll all stop noticing me. This ruddy duck doesn't seem too concerned. He dives again and pops up right in front of me. Is he curious about me? I shiver, even with my sweater and my hood, my two thick shirts, wool socks. Fall is here; the cold, the geese moving, that farmer's stubble burning in the northeast, leaves and marsh turning, the sun falling south again.

I have chosen such a big world for my experiment. In one square foot below me I see a dandelion, Canada thistle, quack grass, alfalfa, a spider. All this life growing with so little care from me. A black beetle scrambles for cover. I feel cold and restless waiting here on my bench. I take a deep breath.

In.

Out.

In.

Out.

That's how the marsh breathes around me. In. And out. Is consciousness everything? When a Buddhist is reborn, what could she do to be reborn a duck? Would life be that bad as a duck?

I step from my bench to the water's edge to study the marsh grass. Cattails, they're easy, a wiener on a roasting stick. Cane grass carries that bushy white broom on top, also called whitetop. But slough sedge, I'm still puzzled, descriptions in my plant book aren't clear enough, I can't tell a lot of these plants apart. A marsh wren chatters beside me. Ernest Thompson Seton, what would he have seen in Manitoba, 1882? Cattails? Cane grass? Passenger pigeons? Eskimo curlews? What are the numbers? How many Manitoba birds have become extinct since then? Was it the hunting? How many species have we hunted to extinction? Whoever said we humans had the right to kill anything?

A flock of smaller passerines chirrups above my head. I see them, hear them, try to tempt them down. *Shpiishh, shpiishh, shpiishh.* Like in the Arctic, they say that if you clap two rocks together the caribou will come and find you. Here, these two rocks, I've tried it, no caribou. But I know that chickadees will come to my call.

I sit on my bench and wait. What is it I'm waiting for, what do I need to know? The shoveller of an hour ago shakes her head. She feeds. Up and down. Up again. Down, up. Turns from east to west. Spins and faces east. That shoveller will probably winter near Mexico, she has a long way to travel, may already have travelled from Alaska. A red-tailed hawk curls around the sky. A scaup jumps from the water, flies a circle in the air, drops again beside his mate. I look over toward the cross, the cormorants are dried and gone, the ruddy duck is gone. A shadow hangs in front of me, my own, the sun is out. I say goodbye to the shoveller, to the ruddy duck, the bench. I leave little behind me. Just the bruised grass, an apple core, a trail of prune pits, a short memory.

I begin the walk back to the car. Suddenly I'm warmer. The moths are too, the sun wakes them, they flutter along the trail. An American bittern flushes in the reeds thirty metres in front of me. Those bitterns—I've discovered another name for them, "look-up"—the way they hold their streaked necks and heads among the reeds, I'd never see them if they didn't move. Water and islands and dikes, and islands and water. Cattails, and sedge grass and water, a nesting tunnel, and water and water. Suddenly, around the bend, two hundred mallards fly up in front of me. I see their markings, dark breast, pale belly, blue patch on the wing. And there, one American black duck among them, much like a female mallard except darker.

Another trail sign, I'll turn to my left, south. I'm going south. I've walked seven kilometres, two to go. These greater yellowlegs so beautiful here in fall, their yellow legs, their spots and bars, their call, their movements. The brown and speckled black-crowned night heron too, stands beside a culvert, hears me coming, flies up. Black-crowned night heron, forty-two species today.

I've left the marsh. Now, on both sides of the trail, prairie, prairie grass, western dock, big bluestem, rust and green and brown. I stop to inspect a flower, a cluster of flowers on a tall stem, still blooming, white sweet-clover, yellow sweet-clover. Not a native plant, sweet-clover may be grown to feed cattle, bees use it to make honey. Pretty flower, perfume. I shield my eyes against the sun and turn to look around me. I love the stretch of this space. I feel an ache for the days when the land was young, before the white man, before the murder of the buffalo, the time of the wild and untamed prairie. I wonder where that image came from, longing for the *old days*, simpler days. Something in the sky behind me! I look up! The pointed wings, black hood of a peregrine falcon far above me. There he is, the fiercest of the hunters, high in the sky above me.

Great egret

Naked and Cold

*H*ere at the Oak Hammock north hill, the marsh and the water reach naked across the cold. I position the car to give me shelter from the weather. Step out, the wind howls around me. I push into a second sweater, tug on my raincoat and pants, two hoods, still cold around my head. Lucky I brought my boots this morning, it's wetter than I expected. Lawn chair and spotting scope on the lee side of the car. I sit. The north hill, my destination for today. Wednesday, October 19; with all my stops and curiosity it's taken more than three hours from home to get here. I'm a lazy man today. I don't plan to walk at all today. I'll just sit here in my chair, huddled against the rain and the weather, I wish I'd thought to bring a lantern though, some kind of fire to set in front of me.

On that day in 1973 when Peter Matthiessen left Long Island to search for the snow leopard in northern Nepal, his Zen teacher took him by the shoulders, bumped Matthiessen's forehead three times with his own, smacked him on the back and then shouted, "Expect nothing!" The wisdom of ages; he should have shouted it to me, I started my first marriage that same year, expectation such an easy way for things to go wrong. The slough grass, brown and dried now, bends before the wind. Cattails stretch and spread and shiver. Dark clouds and sky. I unpack my lunch. Cucumber, tomato, carrot slices, bagels, a pear, a Thermos of coffee, skim milk instead of cream in the coffee—low cholesterol. I'm almost too cold to eat.

By now the rain has stopped. Earlier, the road here to the north hill already so muddy, I might have needed a Jeep or a tow truck to get out. These are the cold days of October. This is the lull before the winter and the storm. The autumn equinox has come, has gone. First frost fell in Winnipeg two weeks ago. The marsh, and the north hill in October, I shouldn't expect much either. But I still do.

The sun had just come up when I left home this morning. Not that I could tell, heavy clouds, I checked the time of sunrise on TV. Drizzle on the windshield. Nine degrees. The wind gusting out of the north-northwest. As I drive to the marsh, even the radio stands against the rules I have set for this game. Mental preparation, the only voices that I hear should be my own, as if that's ever possible. The streets are wet, puddles run against the curb. I take a deep breath, feel the easing in my arms and neck, touch again the pleasure of my self-employment, of not having to work in a factory or an office, work to someone else's moods and orders.

I've always liked rain, the sound, the sight, the feel of it. Inside, watching through an open window. Outside in the puddles, with my yellow raincoat, a sweater, boots, rain all around me, rubber keeping me warm and dry. In the old Dodge pickup with my dad, years ago, on the road to Welland and the market, *slish slish* of the windshield wipers; sometimes in their enthusiasm they *slished* right up onto the roof of the cab. Rain, a change in the tenor of our farm and working life.

Lakes of standing water in the fields, only the tips of stubble pointing. Ditches rushed with water. On Highway 8 I pass a yard where every tree is bare, a hundred trees, more, all empty; naked trunks, a mass of branches, leaves gone. My wish to learn about trees will have to wait till spring. With only branches, bark to guide me, finding names for trees will be far too difficult.

I turn the car off 67 onto the marsh road and watch the shapes of geese and Vs still breaking the sky. Both, snow geese, Canada geese; maybe fewer, five where I saw twenty last time. The weather, this cold north wind, the geese could still be down somewhere in the fields. But not one black-bird. Here at the entrance to the marsh where, this fall, I've watched hundreds of them; the blackbirds are gone. And I do hear guns again. I pass pickups still cluttered on the banks of gravel roads, hay stacked nearby for hunters' blinds. On my right I see a thousand Canadas start from a field of stubble. Left, a thousand snow geese, more, resting on the ground. I wonder for a moment where all these geese came from. The Arctic, I suppose. One location? Would they be the same ones I saw six weeks ago, have they been wait-ing that long? Not likely. A thousand geese, three thousand, maybe ten thousand, more. I love their numbers, I wish there were a million.

This morning's wind seems perfect for the geese to play in. I'm sure they are playing. I watch the snow geese, flash of their long white wings, how they dive, hang and fall, twist and flop, back, forth against the wind. Why do white-winged birds so often have black wing-tips? Matthiessen says that white feathers lack the pigment of black, they are less resistant to wear. Two thousand geese around me, I imagine the colour and the noise, the long hours of daylight, the figures and steps of their Arctic nesting ground.

I lift my binoculars to follow a few ducks in the sky, too high, I can't name them. I trace the wandering of gulls in the summer fallow. Yellow-green legs, black-spotted bills, ring-billed gulls poking their beaks in the mud. I see the flash of shorebird bellies. And here, a yellowlegs, greater, chasing the water's edge. A dozen herring gulls doze on the shore of a pond. A bufflehead dives. Lesser scaups, a northern shoveller, a common goldeneye, a mallard.

When I was still a child, one summer, we tore down our old wooden barn board by board, we really did. We pulled out and straightened all the best nails, then used those boards and nails to frame out a new hip-roof barn that we sheeted in aluminum. The thunder of raindrops on that aluminum roof nothing short of spectacular; you could fix the signature of every single drop. Sometimes I slept in that barn rainy summer nights, and I slept well, the way the downpour rumbled me to sleep. Rain brought both blessing and curse for our farm, good for the crops at the right time, bad at the wrong time, though I never cared that much about crops. The better the crop, the harder we had to work, and I felt we worked too hard anytime. My father and I often stood in the big barn door and dreamed while the rain dusted our noses.

The wind bustles through the willow bluff. Cold. This will be the last day I come without my gloves and winter underwear. An American tree sparrow—clear grey breast, central black dot—flits low in the underbrush. That sparrow makes no complaint about the temperature. A flash of reddish back and tail, a speckled breast, fox sparrow, three of them. One single rusty blackbird steps through a pool. Now with the leaves gone, I see an old nest drooping in a willow. I wonder, a yellow warbler, a chipping sparrow nest? One family of blue-winged teal swims by. Maybe a late brood, the first nest wasn't successful. They're still waiting in October, teal often fly as far south as Peru, what a long way still for them to go. Even the duckweed around them isn't green anymore.

A black-capped chickadee, harbinger of winter in the marsh. *Shpissh shpissh*, I call to the chickadee and it stops on the railing two metres away. Chickadees live in the same general area year-round, will this one wait in the marsh through the winter? Oak Hammock staff do keep winter feeders here in the willows. This ten-gram chickadee will require the equivalent of 250 sunflower seeds a day to survive the coldest Manitoba winter. Apparently, chickadees that live in cold climates replace and enlarge their brains every fall, they need to remember all the places they stash food. When spring and warm weather come, their brain cells begin to die again.

The willows—naked grey, brown—rattle and scrape against each other. A downy woodpecker flashes by, a dark-eyed junco, another rusty blackbird, one remaining common snipe. Finally I have the bluff to myself. No human will dare come for a walk today. Even the hunters will leave the marsh for winter. November, December, January, February, March—the next six months I'll walk in this marsh alone.

I climb back into the car and drive farther along the gravel road toward the north hill. What are those geese? One pink- or orange-legged goose standing with a huge flock of Canadas, a big goose, with a heavy neck. The plumage of the wings and body, breast, just like a Canada goose. The neck is black with white speckles. The forehead white, the cap black, nape white again, a black triangle spots in front of each eye. The bill looks grey and mottled, a bit of orange shines on the mandible. My bird book has no picture for a goose anything like this, but it does mention a greater white-fronted/Canada hybrid.

I pass a Ford pickup, a hunter at the back, orange cap and boots, he throws limp Canada geese over the tailgate. Far in the open field beyond I see a flock of two dozen geese. Heads up and turned into the wind, they look almost as though they're sleeping. I stop the car and raise my binoculars. Puzzling. Very white, very orange bills, should be snow geese but they don't look right somehow. Their behaviour, I've never seen geese act this way, not one of them moving. Suddenly, a man stands in a patch of western dock behind them. A hunter, he wears a camouflage suit, carries a gun, waves his arms and shouts at me. He's angry, I've disturbed

his hunting. I feel laughter pushing at my throat, the geese are decoys and I look like a fool staring at them through my binoculars.

Hunters. All these men with their guns. I'm still upset about hunters, sometimes I wish they'd hunt each other. I think about the early days of hunting, when people lived or died by it, when hunting still mattered. Before guns, before those giant chicken barns on the road to Steinbach. Once, we must have stalked our geese the way the wolves and coyotes do—low in the fields or

Tundra swans

the slough grass; must have chased a goose and taken it by hand, twisted its neck.

Not that many birds at the north edge of this marsh that I can see. Six American tree sparrows dawdle at the foot of the north hill. They settle around me and feed. They fly into the whitetop, I see them up and down among the cattails. They gather beside me again, feed, flutter back into the grass. Four ruddy ducks rest on the water behind them, bills buried in the feathers of their backs. A dozen Canadas call in the hayfield north of the car. An American coot rushes from one stand of sedge grass to another, rushes back and squawks, disappears.

This world is never quite what you think, whether just a few birds, or many. You can change your way of looking. With only one eye to the scope I find the marsh suddenly cluttered with birds, though they shrink and lie low in the curling water. I see ring-billed gulls floating, two of them, and a pack of lesser scaups. I see a flock of mixed geese and ducks, straight-necked tundra swans among them. Those two swans sheltered beside that island swim close enough. I can see the spot of yellow in front of the eye, how the black of the beak reaches the eye in a point and lines straight across the forehead. The gulls beside them, pink-grey legs, must be herring gulls again. A dozen more tundra swans fly up in the south. And there, a group of seven, eight shore-birds on a finger of mud. Hard to name at this distance. At least one is a yellowlegs, lesser, I think. One is much darker than the yellowlegs, brown rather than grey, dark breast and head. Could be a dowitcher. Yes, a dowitcher, nose to the grindstone, the way the bill jabs deep into the mud. Look at the size of that beak. Even these elegant shorebirds are hunters. Most shorebirds feed on animal life, they eat insects and worms, crustaceans, mollusks. Greater yellowlegs love to dine on fish. Be careful, guard your nest, bristle-thighed curlews eat other birds' eggs. Avocets hunt in groups as large as three hundred, herd small fish into shallows where they can easily catch them.

I hear a bubble of song, a western meadowlark. There, three of them, black collars, yellow throat and breast, rest-ing in a naked tree. This is the way the summer dies, with that one song, the meadowlark sings its last note and the marsh folds in all around me. Yesterday, on the phone from Ontario, my father, eighty-five, told me that October has always been a hard month for him, his most difficult month. Probably because of the Depression, he says, how hard it was, he was a young man then. Probably he thinks of dust and drought and autumn, his first daughter who died in those years, her grave, death swarming around him. October; whether he's noticed this since my mother died, I don't know, I never imagined him having difficult months.

I want to tell you how much wonder I feel here in my small wilderness. Sometimes the burden of telling anything at all quashes my shoulders. I would love to tell you how free I feel, how the feeling gathers and spills in my chest; the water, and the rustling grass, and the wind, the geese, the coot, and the tundra swans. I would love to tell you the story of Susan's grandmother, Susan's special grandmother, how close they were. How that grandmother died ten days ago. How she wanted to die. How she begged to die. "This is terrible," she said the last time Susan and I saw her, we visited her in that small room. "No! Worse and worse," she said. "Jesus! God!" She was ninety-one, she'd had a stroke, her meanings weren't very clear anymore. What shame, I was afraid that afternoon to touch her hand. Later she died with no one around her, only a few acquired knick-knacks, we failed to guess the moment. I wish I could tell you that I feel happy.

That one Canada goose sits and squawks in the water; the rest of the flock circles, flaps and circles, straggles south against the sky. One Canada goose deserted on the water. Too old? Too weak to fly any farther? One goose injured, or diseased? My father says that he's not ready to die. He would still much rather start over, be a boy, get married, find a new job. He says old age is lonely, all the friends he had are gone. The few his age that are still alive slump in their wheel-chairs, they don't talk to him anymore. Still, he finds a way to live with courage, some excitement, laughter.

Here's another hunter. A northern harrier flashes above the marsh. The shorebirds fly and curl and drop again, many of *them* will die before the spring. *Tu tu tu.* A greater yel-lowlegs shrieks and runs. Certain groups of Buddhists and Hindus are forbidden to take a life, any life, a mouse, a crow, a mosquito. Life is sacred, that's their teaching. Many Hindus are vegetarian, for the same reason. North Americans are disgusted about the Indian attitude toward cows, that's the first thing they want to talk about in India. What a backward country, how can a cow be sacred?

The seasons shift. An eagle flaps, soars, flaps, soars, thirty metres above the marsh. It circles, rises against the gale. Its fingered wings outline from below, a huge bird, speckled underwing, a young bald eagle. Another eagle, older, this one with a white head and tail, flies to join it.

I sit outside at the north hill for an hour or more. I feel the bitter cold. Then I thaw in the car for a while, drink hot coffee. Suddenly my legs need to walk. Peter Matthiessen wandered for months through Nepal while his son waited for him at home on Long Island. My children, Jonathan and Anna, sixteen and thirteen, are far away, lost in the mountains of northern India, they've travelled there with their mother for a year of school. Their letters tell me very little, that they were alive and well two weeks ago. That trucks still crash on the highway, that the people who died in the plague and the riots lived mostly down on the plains. Two weeks, a millennium in time where children are concerned. What an empty consolation. The Indian telephone never seems to work.

I'm wearing all the clothes I brought. Cotton trousers and shirt. Sweatshirt. A thick sweater. My raincoat and pants, a baseball jacket. Two hoods on my head, a pair of warm socks. Even walking I'm cold. The wind blows and blows, throws up a mallard. The wind rustles in the thistle and the slough grass. The wind storms through the feathers of sparrows. It hisses and pops in my microcassette, I'll hear it again tomorrow at my desk. The wind brushes the grass, sweeps through the whitetop. Here in the northeast the whitetop must be two and a half metres tall, I can't see over it. What a relief to be walking. The wind rushes and whistles, rustles and roars, rattles through trees.

A large round hay bale stands in my path. I'll climb it, look over the whitetop. Oh, in the west, I see forty, sixty tundra swans. These swans seem to live on the edge of winter; they nest high in the Arctic, winter in the United States, I see them only during migration, spring and fall. The wind howls past me. Where does this wind come from? Has it come with the swans from the tundra? The marsh today is mainly wind, the sound of wind, the feel of wind, marsh smell blown around by wind. All you see today is wind, the marsh bending from the wind. The wind whips the slough grass, crowds into my hood, scours my hair. The wind whines and wails, pushes and parts. The wind rolls and ripples, waves along the water. I think buffleheads are probably Susan's favourite duck, she finds them everywhere. Is it their size, how small they are? We saw our first one in Squamish in 1991. Susan should be here with me now. Two dozen buffleheads, white on the face and the wing, flash across the water.

What a long walk, I've brought no map today to guide me. I hike south and east from the north hill to the first dike. I turn and march west. My breath comes in jumps and starts. I walk hard. I started so late today that I'm worried about getting back.

What are these bald eagles hunting? Injured geese, ducks? I've passed clumps of feathers and polished bone along the way. Here, another one, still bloody, a Canada goose for sure, feathers and bones and fluff scattered in a three-metre diameter. All this walking, I'm finally getting warm. A muskrat splashes, paddles from the near shore. Even beavers are killers, I guess, they kill trees. Grass and vegetables are alive, they need to die before we eat them.

Aaaiiyyy aaaaahh, aiiyyyy aaahhh, aaiyyy aahh. Is that the sound of the tundra swan? High low, high low. Yes, there they go, eleven of them. What is this animal dead along the path? Dark brown body, white under the chin, a black tail. Mink. It carries a slash across its back as if from a knife, an eagle's talon. Farther along the trail, I notice the black feces of a dog or a coyote. The mud on the path sucks at my boots, I'm tired, my hips ache. I turn northwest again. I'm glad now that it isn't winter, this weather can't threaten me. I'm lucky not to be Peter Matthiessen, one month's walk from a doctor, high in the Kang La pass. I stop to take off my rubber rain pants, too much resistance against the wind, I watch the hill where I started far to the northeast.

A raven crosses the path in front of me, turns to look at me. Stalks of white and yellow sweet-clover bloom along the trail. And wild alfalfa. I have seen insects today. One, scurrying through the grass when I stopped to urinate against a large rock. Several more when I kicked the remains of bloody goose bone and feather, found bugs crawling on them. Now, on the last quarter of my journey, the wind finally dies and an insect spins the air above me.

I pluck a sample stem of flowers. I shouldn't do that, pick wildflowers, that'll be the last time. Here's one like a cluster of daisies. White rays, a yellow disc, a thumbnail flower, thin inch-long green-grey leaves. Many-flowered aster. Ouch, this one has spines on the leaves. A deep purple ball of flower, nodding-thistle. One thing I've discovered

Red-necked phalarope

here at the marsh, besides the flowers, I enjoy walking. My body, my arms, legs, lungs like to feel utilized, like to work. Finally, the turn in the road, mixed cattle and Herefords crowd around a Texas gate. They all turn to look at me, fifty, sixty head of cattle—cows, this year's calves, steers. My father would have called them. *Co-o boss, co-o boss, co-o-o boss.* I remember the red cow we had at home, Rosie, in the old barn before we built the aluminum one. Rosie made a habit of slipping her halter, jumping over the manger through the window at her head, and running away. We'd come home from church to spend an afternoon hunting for her.

These last few hours I've been skirting the rim of the marsh. Now, a hundred metres away, finally the north hill rises in front of me. Here is my car, I can read the licence plate. I have walked the north loop today. This three-hour walk through the grass and the mud and wind has been exhausting. My clothes are soaked with sweat, I'm going home. What a wonder-filled land. There is a beauty in the marsh, in the rustle and arch of the marsh grass, in the sound of the geese and ducks, in their numbers. I am a hunter too. I have hunted the sixty white swans. I have circled them, studied them from above and below, from each side. I have figured their age, and their strength. I have planned my best strategy, tested the direction of the gale. These old swans. They are old, they have seen the beginning of time. They have attended the birth of the land, the marsh and the land. I have caught beauty in the swans. The wind blows from nowhere, from everywhere. The wind whispers in my ear, I thrill to hear those words. Now, to the south, the first rays of sun break through the day's cloud. It's late afternoon. Today I finally shook hands with the marsh, I heard how it breathed my name. Now I am ready for winter.

Swainson's hawk

Tearing a Dotted Line

Some days I look at the blue sky in the morning and feel like I'm watching it for the first time.

Deep   blue   sky.

I feel glad I got up early. I feel lucky.

A horde of rock doves curves and coils over the railroad yards north of Winnipeg's downtown. Old Arlington Bridge. Have you ever caught the flash of light and colour and the wings of rock doves as they circle in the morning, curl near the railroad track? Sparkle of white and rust, purple and grey, these many-coloured rock doves, the sun flies among them, the sky behind. Have you watched the ring-billed gull waiting in the lot at McDonald's? How it turns, and wheels, settles, jabs a scrap of hamburger, runs, flies up again? Funny how some birds have learned to act almost the way humans do. Here's a crow flapping a crow-line along the street, straight for the south, he seems intent on his goal and destination. The giant Canadian flag at the Perkins Family Restaurant hangs limp against the pole.

November 9. The temperature this morning reads

minus six Celsius, that doesn't matter. The blue-sky sensation is the same, at plus twenty-four, at minus thirty. The forecast is for ten degrees, a south wind, what a beautiful day. Ten degrees, I don't know how we can have this kind of weather in the middle of November, usually we've had our first big snow by now. I'll wake with shock one morning soon, I'll scrape my first shovel of snow and remember about winter. I'll wish I'd stayed outside, deserted work and phone and family, I'll wish I'd stopped this sky-soaked morning in November, stopped and let the moment find me, let the blue sky flood and fill me. This one moment. Sometimes I feel my whole long life trapped in some lonely past, some hopeful future.

I said the sky was blue, that's not quite accurate. It's blue above, and airy, you see the light-years spreading. Have you noticed how it pales, turns grey and hazy, almost brown toward the horizon? Have you seen the colour of the poles, hydro poles, telephone poles, fence? In the morning sun this pole here beside the highway shines almost yellow. The underside of the crossbar is black, here on the back the knots stain dark brown. Did you catch how the sun sparked on the back of that road sign as we chased by? Have you noticed the fields in fall, farmers' fields? Study just this one quarter section: the colour of brown, and dust, and a patch of clover still green, and yellow flowers, black shadows, the shiny blue of ice, more brown. Shiny blue ice? Did you know that ice was blue? Have you seen how the western dock glitters in the rising sun? Now, one heavy lead streak of cloud pencils the west horizon. Have you seen snow geese feeding at sunrise? A luminous white, and many shades of grey. The snow geese fly. Have you ever noticed snow geese black against the sun?

Did you ever examine the world on a sunny morning? Tell me, how did we come to think of colour the way we do, without variation, or shadow? Grass is green. Tree trunks are brown, and hydro poles. Snow geese are white. The sky blue. Sun yellow. Is it only me? Objects have lost their proper colour. They change, the skies change, nothing is fixed, not even colour. Sometimes snow geese turn black, trees turn blue. Even my new red car is red only in one special kind of light.

Do you see that huddle of trees in the distance? This morning, from where I stop on the road, they look black and brown, naked. Do you see that black-billed magpie? Did you even know it had a black bill, that there is a yellow-billed? Black-billed magpie flaps and flutters, flashes the white in its wing, drags its long thin tail behind. Did you start at the gleam of the sun on the southeast quarter of the water tower of the Stony Mountain Penitentiary, a beacon of light? Did you notice the black dome roof beside it? Has your eye tracked the dust from an oncoming car, how it billows and twists, swirls and turns in black and grey from the wheels, how it thickens and hangs and dissipates?

Have you captured the look of geese flying? Sometimes they do fly in Vs. Here, at the Oak Hammock Marsh, Canada geese also fly in check marks and long straggling lines. Geese fly in pairs, in groups or clusters, in capital Ns and catch-all Us. Geese fly in triplets and singles and tick-tack-toes over the roof of the barn here at the marsh entrance. Have you ever watched geese flying? Have you had a good look at this barn? Now, in the morning sun, I understand for the first time the weathered grey faded blue of this hip-roof barn. Blue! A hundred times that I've seen this barn, why has it never shown this colour before?

My friend David once told me that learning to recognize birds is like learning to see. Here I am, I'm forty-five, and learning to see. Where I once saw a duck, or a goose, or a bird, now I see features—a chin strap, a stripe, a slender or hooked beak, a cap or a wing patch, an eye-ring, a colour, the shape of a tail. Have you ever observed herring gulls standing flat on the water on a frosty morning in November? Looks like water. Do you remember the joke about the bird dog that doesn't know how to swim? He trots out instead over the pond to fetch a canvasback for his beaming owner.

We are, all of us, walking on water. Suddenly, now, the hydro poles beside me have turned green. Five hundred Canada geese, heads held erect, white black bums and black legs waggle away from me onto the stubble. Jordan, my nephew, two years old, now that he knows how to run, has no time for anything else, doesn't want anything else. He runs, and runs. He sleeps. Runs. Where does he get that desire? Today, I feel just like that, so busy, looking and looking.

The second of the three Oak Hammock loops north of the interpretive centre stretches the longest, that's my walk for today. I gather my sack to my shoulder. I scan the horizon. The marsh and the prairie this morning describe an encyclopedia of brown, and gold, and grey. Two white spots on a ridge a half mile to the west, I lift my binoculars, rocks in the morning light, the snowy owls will be there soon. I walk from the car, swing around after fifty paces and catch a glare in my headlights. Alarm! The battery, what would I do out here with a dead battery? Then I realize it's only the sun. *Only* the sun . . .

Here in the dried mud on that long second trail I see footprints. A dog? A coyote? This one. See how neatly it divides into toes and claws, a pad. What does a coyote print look like? Is that coyote somewhere nearby? Is it downwind, can it smell me? Wind? The south wind that was forecast for this morning hasn't arrived yet. Small tufts of white blossom on a channel of ice, the ice shades into brown and black, green and grey from where I walk. I watch my shadow in the morning, how it wanders behind me, how it stretches and blurs on the edges. I hear a twitter in the reeds, some small group of passerines waiting for morning warmth in the marsh while it rests and feeds.

Have you taken the time to kneel, survey the conference of frost on a stalk of slough grass? Square foot of slough grass? Frost gathers in jags and crystals and needles. This thin two-inch stem of growth at my feet has hundreds of millimetre balls of ice crammed along it, a landscape in miniature. Once you get down this low, nose to the ground, you find bits of yellow and green hiding too. I get up, walk farther, the frost hisses beneath my boots. That small rock, half buried in mud, shines like gold in the morning sun. I am a miner, my pan and my hammer, my Klondike, that rock earns my interest. I feel like a rich man.

I listen for the hum of a truck, the whisper of geese, the murmur of life far in the distance. Here at the first turn of my trail, quiet rests on the marsh all around me. I consider the black-crowned night heron I startled at this same spot a month ago. Where is that heron today? Alive, I hope. Surely it's flown far to the south, may be in Texas already. Did it follow the same route Susan and I took to Corpus Christi? One mottled mallard lifts from the marsh and whistles into the east. I feel the nudge of the wind waking. I hear the call of another small bird in the cattails, maybe a shorebird, old or injured, deserted here to the winter. I stand trapped on the banks of this marsh, I can't follow, can't find it.

Have you watched how the muskrat pokes his dark nose through the ice? How he climbs up without breaking any more of the surface? Have you watched how he shakes himself, how the water drops glaze in the sun? Muskrat sits in the shadow of slough grass and sedge. His humped body bristles with whiskers and brusque individual hairs. Muskrat's coat colours in compounds of grey, rust and tan. Front feet up, near his mouth, he chews on a brown reed. "Hello, muskrat." I'd like to call to him, get his attention. Instead, I just sit and watch for a while from behind the grasses, twenty-five metres away. Finally I get up. The next time that muskrat turns, looks in this direction, I'll be gone, I'll be hiding farther in the marsh. Maybe I'll have found an eagle.

An eagle. There. Bald eagle, circle and flap and circle. What's that eagle looking for? Why is it waiting? What is its name? Where was it born and how many miles has it flown since it fledged there? Where will it spend the winter? The night? Is it healthy? How long will it live? When was its last meal? Does it have friends? Do eagles keep friends? So many questions, I wish it could answer. I watch the bald eagle, tail and underwings blotched from below. Circle. Flap and circle. Swoop. Friends. I see four more eagles, only one with the white head and tail, yellow bill of an adult. Have you seen how an eagle's white head and tail glimmer in the sun? As you walked by, eyes still on the adult and glimmering eagle, did you notice this cluster of muskrat huts, lodges? Two, three, seven, ten, all within thirty metres of me. A muskrat town exposed. Have you ever visited a muskrat town? In summer most of these huts would have hidden deep in the grass. Look. In the reeds. A muskrat. Smash! A hole in the ice. Is gone.

Have you seen how the water freezes in waves and swirls and channels, in ridges and ripples, in bubbles? How it lumps and bumps, glasses and flakes? How it freezes in sheets and circles and patches, leaving small pools of water to run in the south wind? Have you watched how the ice gleams and slow dances, how it dazzles the bright waiting sun?

Northern shoveller

Here at the bench where I lunched weeks ago, flocks of ducks gather in the water, on the ice at the foot of the cormorant cross, the cross of the black drying wing-stretched cormorants. The cormorants are gone, long ago. The wooden cross reaches naked in the flood, only the swallow house still nailed to its stem. The ducks remain nameless to me, dark shapes flying into the light. These ducks seem so fearful today. Restless, I can't get close enough to see them. Is it the ice, do they feel vulnerable because of the ice, predators trotting across the ice? Is it eagles, the memory of guns and hunters? I have caught the shape of a lesser scaup, I think, the bill of a shoveller. Those look like mallards, that flock. Here at the centre of the marsh thousands of ducks still stage for their journey south.

This one pack of ducks isn't as easily frightened. I take ten steps, and study, a bufflehead. Ten more steps, and study, a pintail. I guess the curve of this trail is just right, these ducks feel that I'm not getting closer. Ten more steps, a common goldeneye. I feel bold with my success, take fifteen steps, they haven't flown yet. Those small ducks closest to me must be green-winged teal. A pair of canvasbacks. A dozen more buffleheads. A redhead, two.

Have you noticed how ducks fly off the water? How one starts and the rest fly up in quick procession, almost like tearing a dotted line, ducks one way, liquid the other. The Buddhist monk, if he truly wishes to find enlightenment— or she, there must be women monks by now—must shed all his/her possessions. Tearing a dotted line. Sometimes less means more; for the ducks, more sky, less water. A paring down. One pair of boots. One pair of pants. A shirt, two books, one old harmonica, a knapsack. Too much? Anna, her golden hair, what will she bring from India, what will she leave behind? What does an eagle carry? At forty-five I still find myself collecting. For what? *Aaaiiyyy aaaaahh, aiiyyyy aaahhh, aaiyyy aahh*, I hear tundra swans somewhere ahead of me over the ice.

This trail I walk along has been used recently by

vehicles. It's a dike actually, wide, quite high, has two vehicle ruts. Have you seen those red cotton ribbons, beside the muskrat holes? Those are the marks of trappers. I just met one, a trapper. He's out there with his skiff and his waders, his paddle. He's stranded, half on, half off the ice. He breaks large sheets of it, shakes up his traps while his van idles on the dike. He says it's too warm for trapping muskrats this fall. "Damn weather"; he brings up another trap. And the prices are low, he says. "I'll wait until next year," he says, "next year will surely be colder."

This is the way the morning passes. Sun in the sky. Crystals of cloud—cirrus, high, thin, and light—they gather, shift, fade. The sedge grass bends. Feathers scatter along the path, tremble with the wind. A hundred, two hundred tundra swans shadow the ice. And a trapper. Have you watched how the morning passes? I crouch in the grass as a northern harrier wings its way from the north, straight toward me. Long narrow wings, round tips, a female. I hope she'll fly right over me. I want her to fly right over me. I settle lower in the grass. I'm just another quiet piece of marsh. Come, big harrier, fly right through me. But she curls to the west instead, must have seen me, maybe heard me, too busy thinking. Harrier, spot of white rump, disappears against the horizon. I've walked about five kilometres. I stop, I play dog, leave my mark at the base of a signpost. Silly, I know. But maybe that coyote will pass here tomorrow, maybe he'll pause, raise his nose to the air, maybe tomorrow that coyote will think about me.

The wind stretches. Slough grass rustles. Suddenly I feel cold. I'm beginning to understand why people talk so much about the weather. Everything here in the marsh depends on the weather. Wind, sun, cloud, rain. Flood or drought. Weather is gentle, is cruel. Weather pushes against you. This marsh, the stage weather acts upon. Theatre. The curtain rises, the weather hits you solid, weather is physical. What do you notice first, the weather, or the earth you stand on? Our lives depend completely on the weather. Whether the car starts. Whether you get a snowy holiday from work.

How you dress. How your mood sags after a week of rain and cloud. How the sun wakes you at five in the morning in summer. How your body glows on a warm day. How you lose sleep during a heat wave. One man here in Steinbach, Manitoba—Ben Friesen, maybe—remembers the weather for every day since he was born. Ask him. He'll tell you. "November 9, 1953. That was a cold and stormy day, four inches of snow."

Water, grass, trees in the distance. Have you watched how the earth reaches deep into the horizon? These islands here, see how they're spaced, almost planted, footholds across the water. I catch the twitter and *chir-r* of small birds again. Are they some kind of longspur, I wish I could see them. Here they are, right above me. Brown bodies, some with black tails, facial stripes, they're the size of horned larks. Are they longspurs? Oh, white wings when the sun shines through, and black tips, a flock of snow buntings. Maybe a horned lark or two among them, I know that buntings and horned larks fly together in winter. I watch as they fly, as they flutter and bob, pause in the air, as they weave, lift and fall. They fly over me. They turn. They fly to the left. Turn again. I lose sight of them finally just where I first picked them up.

Time flows when you're walking, just seems to turn in the marsh, walking. One hour, two hours, three pass in a matter of minutes, I'm glad I'm out here. Clocks crawl so slowly in a house, in cramped quarters, tick, tick, when you're lying at night and worried, when you hear a mosquito in the dark. I haven't seen any insects today, but they're here, I suppose, in the soil, in the mud below the water. What does Annie Dillard say? 1,356 creatures—mites, springtails, millipedes—live in the top inch of every square foot of forest soil. How does she know that? Did she take a spade? Did she dig up and count? I wonder who actually counted. This marsh holds far more life than I ever imagined. That's what surprises me about the marsh, and about the prairie, maybe they're just as scenic as the mountains. You need to pay attention, get right down on your hands and knees. My dad says those mountain-lovers have no imagination. Mountains are beautiful, but sometimes, when you look at them, they're so big they block out everything else. My dad prefers the marsh and the prairie.

Our fruit farm was never good enough for me. Seven acres? My ten-year-old fantasies demanded a section, or two. A herd of cattle, a horse, a combine. I cut coupons out of farming magazines. I filled in my name and address. I begged a dime and a stamp and sent away for bulletins on sheep shearing, on new breeds of cattle, on the latest farming technologies. I kept scrapbooks, I thought I belonged on the prairie. In August, the middle of peach season, salesmen would idle up our farm drive in Niagara hoping to sell us machinery. They looked puzzled, why had we written? What did we want with a baler, a swather, that big four-wheel-drive tractor, on a seven-acre fruit farm? My father got tired always having to explain.

Two, four miles distant, I see a tractor. Out on the prairie tractors sometimes look as tall and far away as elevators. Light rays bending, a mirage. Or is that an elevator? I reach for my binoculars. It moves, pivots, red and yellow, a tractor, in this one moment the life of a farmer passes before me. The farmer ploughs. He tills. He seeds. He drives his tractor across last summer's wheat field, drives from east to west to east. Spring, summer, fall. Year after year. Two sections of land, a childhood dream, I feel myself in the tractor beside him, rumble and stink. That row of aluminum granaries must mark his yard, and the trees, the house hidden behind them. His wife and business partner probably waits in the kitchen with the calculator. Soon she'll have to pick up the kids at school. She punches at the calculator again, the cost of a year's supply of groceries, the price of a funeral. Someone has died. His mother? His father? A dream? The end of the family farm? I think about Christmas and crops and gifts for my children, the carton of chocolate bars I packaged for faraway India. Emotion runs flat as the grass around me. Just like the mallard that starts when I walk by, just like the woman with the calculator, I too worry about the future; three of us share that kernel of grandeur, the passing of time. I study the lines in the palm of my hand, where are their scars and secrets?

The mystery of a swan. There. That swan waits for me. It turns. Watches. Stretches its neck, watches. One grey swan, even the bill coloured grey. It stands belly deep in the water, steps from its hole in the ice, from its watery hole onto the ice. Paddles, runs. Stretches its wings. Flaps, runs, flaps. Flies deeper into the marsh. Here, a Canada goose dragging its wing on the ice. It runs too, staggers and slips. It calls, anticipates evening and eagles. These shovellers in the corner of the pond to the left of me, bright orange legs, white-breasted males, brown mottled females, they've let me come this close. I've hidden and tricked them. They think that I'm whitetop, cane grass, I stand tall against the sun with the whitetop. To my right, more ducks, they see me, I hear applause, a roar of wings, the sound of two thousand wings flapping.

Have you seen how the marsh sprawls and swells before you? Water, and grass. And grass, and water and grass. Ice. Grass and ice. I walk through the ages and ice. I blunder from path, to dike, to path again. I meet answers, more questions. I find memory. I am hungry for food, and for love. I walk through time, and the marsh. I fondle the grass. I kick at the goose droppings and feces around me. I have tasted freedom and wisdom, here on the trail, and loss. I've found feathers and fur and corpses in my path. I have seen the wind, how it raced by me. I have heard fear in the flight of a mallard. I have brought death all around me, and some life.

This is the mystery of food and digestion, the wonder of rhythm and hunger and birth. Does it sound like I'm bragging? Do you think that I'm bragging? I have a right to brag. I am here. I'm alive. This is how I feel. I feel how my legs ache after a ten-kilometre walk.

Just now, here, I wish I could find a bench somewhere along the way.

Western meadowlark

Open Spaces

*T*he world looks ragged, white and brown, dried slough grass and snow, here at the early edge of winter. That grey string of trees scattered in the distance the single mark between this heavy earth and sky—where does one leave off, the other begin? A desolate and beautiful landscape.

I haven't visited the marsh in over a month. One week I tossed in bed with the flu. The next, I nursed a broken toe, crashed it while helping a friend move. Third week, business and an outing with a friend in Victoria. Work, and pain, and pleasure. A whole month since my last marsh eagle; my last tundra swan or bufflehead, goldeneye or pintail; since the last snow and Canada geese I pondered feeding among the grasses—though I did catch a glimpse of four black turnstones on the rocky shores of Vancouver Island. Turnstone, from its habit of turning over rocks and shells and weed in its search for food; my first black turnstones, white belly, dark and light pied wings in flight. Cold. It's turned cold here in Manitoba since I returned, the last two weeks at minus twenty-five Celsius. Today, though, the weather has broken; at six this morning it was already up to seven below. The winter solstice, Christmas, just about a week away.

I plan to work hard for birds today. I'd like to see ten or fifteen species. Is that even possible at the marsh in December? An owl, snowy. Chickadee, nuthatch and woodpecker around the feeder. Raven, magpie, maybe a Canada goose. Some kind of duck at the artesian well on the marsh west boundary. A rough-legged hawk, a snow bunting. Probably a house sparrow in the shrubs round the main building. I don't know, it sounds difficult. The first species, a giant raven, flaps above me into the southwest. The snow crunches on the boardwalk, crumples under my feet. The marsh blows cold even sheltered in the willow bluff, even at minus seven Celsius. A south wind pulls hard at my ears and face.

I find rabbit tracks all around me, crowded and running in every direction, as though the local rabbits just held a community meeting, they must have been busy overnight. Could have been only one, I suppose, they say single rabbits do that, make these bunches of track. How can I describe this rabbit track? A cluster of four prints—two small, two large prints—almost a capital T. Or the mathematical pi even better, the four-footed pi of a rabbit trail. Irrational number, just like this marsh for me. Oak Hammock has two types of rabbits, I've seen them. White-tailed jackrabbit, eastern cottontail, big and small. Eastern cottontail females often mate within three days of the birth of a litter. Might even have snowshoe hares here, I haven't seen those, but one of the Oak Hammock staff thinks maybe she has.

Rabbits. My father often reminded me of his hunting experience on the prairie as a young man, how one jackrabbit screamed when he shot it, a human sound, he never hunted again. We did raise and butcher pigs and steers and chickens on the farm when I was young, that never seemed to bother him; somehow my father thought rabbits were different, maybe because they were wild, independent. Rabbits have the peculiar habit of recycling their own droppings, eating them, they seem to gain added nutrients. How would they have learned that? Natural selection, I suppose, they learn it from their parents. Maybe not that peculiar a habit; I think other mammals sometimes eat the droppings of their young, deer to protect their fawns from predators. Some humans drink their own urine, they think it improves their health. I learned about rabbits long ago, I must have been quite enterprising as a young man. At sixteen I already kept a hutch full of rabbits, my own little rabbit farm. Chinchilla, New Zealand, buck and doe. I bought and bred and sold rabbits for the commercial meat market, an early education in both reproduction and economics; I never made any money. These marsh rabbits have all deserted their tracks, hidden somewhere from the light, burrowed into a snow-drift. I stoop to try and catch a familiar scent, I listen for them rustling.

I can't find any coots or yellowlegs, any teal or snipe. No geese call. No muskrats push up through the black ice. Not even rabbits anywhere that I can see. The marsh lies abandoned. Looks abandoned—I know frogs and insects sleep somewhere in the frozen mud. There, one lonely magpie arches and stutters into the trees, spreads its long black arrow-tail. One raven, one magpie, the only life left in the marsh today. Maybe today I'll study the magpie, the beautiful black-billed magpie, tell you a story of the magpie.

Black may seem a simple word, the absence of colour. The magpie's head, neck, upper breast, back and tail are black. But they carry a gloss of bronze and green and purple hues. The abdomen and wing patches are white. Its long tail and flight, the contrast of black to white to black again, give the magpie a particularly elegant appearance. And the five-foot domed magpie nest introduces a new category of bird mansion, magpies nest inside, under cover; the outer surface of coarse sticks and prickles and twigs, the cup of delicate plant stems and horsehair. According to my bird encyclopedia magpies eat flies and grasshoppers, larvae and ticks, grain and small mammals. They belong to the family of bird scavengers, they clean carcasses off the side of the road. Still, it seems that the black-billed magpie is one of the most hated birds in North America, we humans seem to hate scavengers, farmers often kill magpies claiming to protect their crops and livestock.

Tony Angell writes about a crow roost in Illinois earlier this century that was hung with one thousand shrapnel grenades while the birds were out feeding. When the crows returned for night the grenades were detonated. In the morning, so the story goes, 100,000 dead crows lay on the ground. For the sake of farm crops and livestock. Farming, Angell argues, is the most environmentally destructive activity humankind has ever been involved in.

Solitary sandpiper

I walk, and rest. Walk again across the snow. Rest. My poor half-mended toe has brought me the short way back to the willow bluff. Here, empty barn swallow nests nuzzle the wall under the eaves of an outbuilding. Four or five sunflower seed feeders, a suet bag and branch hang deserted. I sit and wait. And wait. No one comes, no thing, no creature. I wait. Five minutes. Ten. Fifteen. Suddenly, a black-capped chickadee whistles behind me. The chickadee flits to one of the feeders—head, tail, bob and jerk, a nervous-looking bird—picks up a seed, darts into the bush. Chickadees, though they seem fidgety, can be quite friendly with people, I've had them eat out of my hand. Another chickadee arrives. It too takes a seed into the willow, knocks the seed against a branch to crack it, works hard to finally break that sunflower open. Two chickadees, feeder to willow to feeder, just as suddenly they're gone. I wait again. I think of Peter Matthiessen watching for the snow leopard in Nepal, he waited for weeks in his tent, months. I imagine the warblers, the sparrows, ducks, thrushes I saw here in the willow bluff last summer. I could stay and watch for them, long time until they come again, I could wait here for two children.

There, a downy woodpecker chants deep into the wind. Four hours, how long I've been here, and four bird species. I sit cross-legged on the wooden decking, back straight against a post, my throat groans with the marsh's desolation. Solitude. A Buddhist meditation. Like the woodpecker, black and white. Chop wood, carry water, chop and carry, brew tea. A cautious rhythm. I sit alone. And I sit alone. This is the marsh and the mantra of absence. Absence, they say, makes the heart grow. Grow what? Silent? Anxious?

Like my father, I have enjoyed the antics of crows. Their rock and cough and *caawww* on the street lamp. Their hundred thousand autumn crow conventions, Saskatoon. Their windy roll and flop and joggle while in flight. Their quarrels along the roadside over a bloody piece of mouse. Just last spring I watched as two dozen crows flew screaming and mobbing over my city house after an owl they'd found somewhere perched in an evergreen. What a commotion, every songbird parent within a mile must have known about that owl, the danger. Owl chase, wild crow chase. Those crows dragged me four blocks south, two east, five city blocks north, two south again, till my legs, lungs, heart, body felt half-dead—I just wanted to get a better look at my first great horned owl of the season.

I don't know much about the occurrence of artesian springs on the North American prairie. They bubble up through shifted layers of rock from far below, water that's percolated down through sandstone, apparently they're not uncommon, Oak Hammock Marsh has one. I drive west and north from the willows to see it. I hope I'll find ducks there sheltered from the winter. There! Look! Water gurgling from the ground in the thick of a Manitoba winter, after two weeks of minus twenty-five Celsius. Open water. A pool of it, clear, a metre deep, some kind of marine weed still green and floating at the water's edge, mist rising. I walk east along the stream as it leads back toward the centre of the marsh. Five minutes. This shallow pebbled stream, by now less than a foot deep, after all that arctic air still holds its liquid memory of summer. I walk, and walk. No ducks, but the tracks of a dog or coyote running here beside me. How far does this stream reach? How far is it open? Five hundred, a thousand metres? I'll weigh its length. Soon I'll turn around, when I reach that bush, on the way back I'll count my steps.

52, 53, 54, 55, 56 . . . Prints of two smaller mammals now scratched in the snow beside me. Beware small mammal, beware the coyote.

198, 199, 200, 201, 202 . . . This is a landscape of two, three. The sky, the snow, my body. A least perspective.

323, 324, 325 . . . Snow begins to fall, heavy. The distance disappears, the trees in the distance disappear. I can't see. Only the reeds and rushes, cattails, here, three metres in front of me. That muskrat, hunched, racing across the ice and snow. Downwind, he must have smelled me coming.

506, 507, still counting steps . . . The flat earth. A shrinking universe of snow. One human spot in a pale continuum. I lift a hand in front of me, I can't tell anymore; do I see for miles into the distance, or has a curtain fallen across my eyes?

December. A few years ago, just after Christmas, Susan and I set out to drive to British Columbia, she needed to start her job there the first week in January. Minus thirty-four when we left Winnipeg in the dark and early morning, Celsius, dangerous time for a drive. We counted the miles to Brandon, breakfasted there at the Petro-Can. Back in the car about sunrise, we turned on the radio, a voice told us the mercury had fallen to minus thirty-nine. The water temperature gauge on our dashboard wouldn't budge, the heater blew cold air. Susan sat quiet beside me, hands gloved, wisp of brown-grey hair showing from under her toque and hood. Cold frost and fog gathered all along that highway, we threw blankets over our knees, talked comfort to each other. What a relief, finally, when the temperature jumped into the teens near Regina.

701, 702, 703 . . . I can hear the water again bubbling from the spring.

Magpies, crows, ravens. Where did they get their evil reputations? What do I know about the raven? That it's black, and cunning—clever may be a less poisoned word. That it's bigger than a crow, has a wedge-shaped tail and shaggy throat feathers. That it fed Elijah in the wilderness. That it haunted Poe. That it brought light and order to the homes of aboriginal Americans. Long, long ago, when the people of the first winter died because they had no fur or feathers, raven brought fire to save them. Why did those early Americans choose the raven for their story? Because it was predictable? Because it was always there, even in winter? The solace of a raven's call. My second raven, there, eating something in the middle of that field, pecking and pulling at a carcass. Black, and a white field.

What is it about winter that we find so beautiful? Why does this landscape pull at our bones? A spectacle of freezing, of thirty below, of cold and wind. *Until hell freezes over.* A pageant of desolation, of death, of the end of things. A cinema of sleep, of peace. Preview of the apocalypse. What are the poetics of this winter marsh? Now, at two in the afternoon, suddenly the sun wakes, a yellow glare behind a cloud. Gretel Ehrlich, in *The Solace of Open Spaces*, writes about her ranch life in Wyoming. All this space, she says, reminds me of possibility. Maybe winter is like that, it reminds you of spring.

I'd like to sing about the solace of open spaces. There is a consolation here if you can see it. This quiet carries its own gravity, it settles you down. You see the marsh has changed, autumn to winter, will always change, you feel comforted. Land and heaven blend into one horizon, one pale grey horizon. No eagles, no rough-legged hawks, no snowy owls, only empty fence posts. Still, those fence posts hold a promise of their own, someday a hawk will rest there. You see justice too. The damage we do will be short-lived, we'll never outlast it. Fossil records tell us that ninety-nine percent of all the species that ever lived on earth are now extinct. One day our sun too will flicker and die, will shape our retribution. If you wait that long in the cold you will die.

Another short drive before I stop at the Oak Hammock north hill. I step from the car. I hear the sound of thunder, thunder and snow, like that day in August when I straddled my horse in a thunder snowstorm on a ridge high above the town of Jasper, I couldn't believe that thunder and snow would mix. I feel the wind in my hair, in my ear, the wind chanting in my ear. I sit on a bench. This marsh reaches far up into the sky, the slough grass points toward a distant planet. I walk again. The snow slushes under my boots. It seems my words are bound to the creatures I long for, to the creatures I know, the distance I can see. I wish I could write the mysteries of rock and feeling and fossil. Peter

Matthiessen? Did he ever see that snow leopard? I just can't remember, I don't think so. His dreams, his four months waiting. Maybe some dreams are better left open and unfulfilled.

Greater yellowlegs (above) and lesser yellowlegs (below)

Hoping for a Miracle

Winter! What a long hard winter this year in Manitoba! Record depths of snow, fifty percent more than usual. Record low temperatures. Cold, the coldest cold of the century. And snow on the ground far longer than usual, late into April, winter records coming again and again. I found myself complaining about the weather. Thinking too much about the weather. Every time it turned cold or snowed I told Susan, "This'll be the last time for sure. That's a promise. I grew up on a farm," I said, "I should know the weather." I woke up the next morning discouraged, I didn't like to get out of bed, when winter drags that long everybody gets discouraged. I kept talking about Arizona, that we should have travelled to Arizona in February. I heard on the radio news about Montreal's recent ad campaign: "Think you don't like Montreal? Have you tried Winnipeg?" What a long and terrible winter.

By mid-April I thought spring had come to Manitoba. Temperatures spun from minus twenty to plus ten degrees Celsius in seven days, the snow finally beginning to melt.

The Red and Assiniboine Rivers began to rise, ice cracking and opening and breaking, jamming along the river shore, both Red and Assiniboine spilling their banks. And the birds. The birds moving, crying. Canada geese in chevrons in the morning over the city. Golden eagles, bald eagles, rough-legged hawks. Sharp-shinned hawks, kestrels, northern harriers, broad-winged hawks. One hundred and forty-three red-tailed hawks in ninety minutes at the St. Adolphe bridge just south of Winnipeg—I waited with a group of twenty other birders on that bridge—hawks coming so fast over the trees sometimes it was difficult to call and count them. Robin, redpoll, red-winged blackbird, purple finch, mourning dove, northern flicker, song sparrow, yellow-rumped warbler. All these and twenty other spring species of birds passing by the house in one flown and feathered morning.

If I were to tell you the truth about that mid-April, I'd say the excitement soaked deep into my toes. Every spring somehow feels like the first one. Finally, after all those tiresome days of winter, after the cold and the snow, I could open the back door and walk right into spring. I drove out to the marsh. I was hoping for a miracle, as though the birds weren't enough. Maybe a brave blue flower. Maybe a fox, cousin to the one that played with Eiseley in the prow of that beached boat on the New England shore. Maybe a comet, another Hyakutake, swinging its sparked tail across my dark and night sky. Some small and singular inspiration, a clue to the riddle of those sad stone faces on Easter Island. Just one simple miracle.

Water. I drove through water. Overnight Manitoba had turned into one big lake. Farmers' fields stubbled and covered in water. Ditches full to the gravel edge of the road with water. Houses hemmed in with sandbags and mud, quick dams and dikes and barricades. Here and there, only a few leftover points or jags of snow. I turned on the wipers, it was beginning to drizzle. What did my instructors teach me in secondary school, that rain revitalized the earth, we were probably studying British poetry. What did I learn in my archaeology class at the university? People used to believe that rain was the semen that made things grow. Don't Manitoba farmers always wish for rain in spring, something to get the crops going? What a wonder! The first spring drizzle!

Ten minutes later at Oak Hammock Marsh, the world still seemed three-quarters frozen. A few geese had gathered in twos and threes, and some mallards, the northern pintail and his mate. A scattering of song sparrows, juncos, American tree sparrows huddled and sulked in the under-brush. A red-winged blackbird poked at the one remaining bag of suet. A single fox sparrow shivered his song from a sapling, in the distance a killdeer's lonely cry. The magpie pair called its old question: *What? What? What?* The marsh lay dried and rustled, stiff and cold. I felt like that old February groundhog in Pennsylvania, despite the cloud and rain, anxious to crawl deep inside my hole again.

I walked. And I walked. And walked. What else could I do out there on my ten-kilometre trail, there was nothing to see. I rehearsed the subjects of the last few weeks: that late party, my friends, my age, my work. My age, I have begun to notice when people around me die, that friends die. I thought about my health, my heart, sometimes I'm not so sure anymore. Sometimes when I'm out here at the marsh I wonder why people work so hard. Why do I work so hard? A bigger house? A more fashionable car? Big-screen TV? What is it we'll need when we're old and ready to die? Sometimes I feel old and almost ready to die. How many cars do I need between now and when I'm eighty? That crazy *one more house and car* cliché. I felt oddly frightened out there in the cold, out on my trail in the wind and cold at the back edge of winter. What if I got sick and couldn't walk back? I remembered Dr. Robillard last visit saying that my blood was a bit low on iron, she told me to take some pills, maybe I'd come out too soon. My age? Forty-six isn't that old.

I noticed feces out on the trail. What kind of animal? Big enough for a dog, a coyote, bush wolf. And prints of a split hoof . . . A deer? This deep in the marsh? The nearest trees at least three kilometres away. The track didn't seem quite right for deer, too deep, and short. Still, with the harsh winter, and the depth of snow, I'd heard that deer were coming far into the open to feed. I noticed a rough-legged hawk high in the air above me, and then falling, down along the patchwork of snow. And those feces again, I took a kick at them. Dry enough now, just skin and fur, some coyote must have had jackrabbit for its winter meal. I felt vulnerable out there on the trail. I looked behind to see if a wolf might be following me. I know, there are no wolves in the marsh, or anywhere on the prairie, but I couldn't help looking anyway.

I walked. I thought about my work, about writing. That was my purpose out here in the marsh, to write about it. Who would have chosen such a life, a writer's life? You write. And you write. One page today, one page tomorrow, the day after. Nothing much happens. You hope to hone your skill. You hope your words will reach an audience. You hope, someday, to find some recognition. Out in the open, those deer, easy prey for poachers. I've never hunted. An accident? Maybe. I like deer and moose well enough on the barbecue. But I don't long to pull a trigger. I don't wish to kill animals, geese, bears, elk; maybe the odd dog at home that wanders into my backyard. I have thought, though, about the pleasure of sitting with a friend or a cousin in a duck blind, sunrise, in fall, with a doughnut and a cup of Thermos coffee. Suddenly, out in the marsh, I caught myself singing a lullaby, prairie lullaby, song about cattle and stars and campfires.

That marsh day in April the news was full of flood, roads and bridges washed out all over southern Manitoba. I drove home along the Red River, south from Selkirk, the river swollen and packed with ice. River pushing across patios, bumping down into basements, creeping into kitchens. Red River; two-by-fours and bits of plywood, a

American avocets

billboard, fence posts and dead trees, islands of branch and ice, gliding down the river. I drove into Winnipeg along Highway 9 south of Lockport, the snow started to drift lazy across the road. The wonder of nature, I thought, the wonder of ice and the thaw. This is the wonder of rivers. The marvel of heavy falling snow, another ten centimetres of heavy snow. Here, the wonder of Manitoba weather, always a surprise. Snow again! I had begun to feel quite unhappy.

Back in my warm living room later I read an article in the newspaper, it quoted a spokeswoman from the United Nations. She said that 150 species of life become extinct every twenty-four hours, that tropical forests are disappearing, that air pollution is increasing. I read about the ozone hole and about water shortages and acid rain. That news filled me with a deep sorrow. I thought about the earth, our planet earth. I still find this earth so beautiful, but sometimes I'm afraid it won't survive much longer. I thought about us, our species—humans—do we even have a chance to survive? If we do, will there be any other life left around us?

In early May, a friend from the Canadian Wildlife Service and I went on a woodcock survey. Yes, exactly the way it sounds, we went to count woodcocks. A sandpiper of marshy thickets; the only one I've seen my neighbour found dead in his yard last year, I held it in my hand, must have crashed against a window. The male American woodcock performs his courtship flight at dawn and at dusk. He flies up in a long spiral, wings whistling, to a height of three hundred feet; then he zigzags like an autumn leaf back to the ground where the female waits to mate with him. The woodcock can be hunted in fall and is apparently quite tasty; the count helps to monitor each year's hunting. That survey gave my spine a jingle.

Eastern Manitoba, out in the Whiteshell, Fire Road 13, a good omen I guess. The sky shone perfectly clear. We marked time at our starting point until exactly twenty-two minutes after sunset, latitude, longitude, someone had done the precise calculation. We got out of the truck. We listened, we expected to hear the male call toward the end of his flight, when he approached the female. Two minutes. No woodcocks. We got back in the truck and drove .6 kilometres. We stopped. We listened. Two minutes. No woodcocks. We drove again. We stopped. Drove and stopped. And I noticed then that the moon was beginning to break over the trees. A full moon. I forgot about woodcocks for a moment and fixed my binoculars on the moon. Talk about miracles. Does that moon glimmer and glow when you look at it through binoculars. Does that moon jump when you watch with your binoculars, you can see all its trails and mountains and plains.

On our seventh stop, there, the sound of a woodcock. Ron and I smiled our excitement and shook hands. There, again. And a second woodcock a bit farther north. We drove. Our eighth stop, two more woodcocks. On our tenth stop, last stop, our world suddenly spun upside down. We stood on the road, two of us, just the two of us, and the full moon at our backs, an hour after sunset. The earth spun with sound, noisy with sound. Chorus frogs sang in the ditches. Wood frogs burped from the brush. Mallards *quawk quawk quawked* above our heads so close my instinct and body shouted to crouch. One robin, loud in the northwest. The rattle of a sandhill crane far away. A ruffed grouse drummed. Common snipe twittered and twisted and winnowed through the night. Here, the *peent* of a woodcock. There, another. A third. And the male's whistling flight. It was dark, already dark. My miracle. My hands shook.

In mid-May the streams and ditches around the marsh filled with waterfowl—gadwall, redhead, shoveller, teal. The sky chittered with tree and cliff and barn swallows, the call of song and clay-coloured sparrows. Red-winged blackbirds sang again, like last year, their symphony in the slough grass and cattails. I drove along gravel roads. I passed through a Texas gate and a meadow into the middle of a herd of sixty horses, mares, and two dozen foals. Running, bucking foals. Sleeping foals. Sucking foals. Curious foals. But most of the mares still slow and heavy and waiting.

I stopped the car and pulled on my rubber boots, wandered across the wet meadow into the cold. I watched the grass begin to green, even through the water. Here and there, bugs, insects flew up from below and rested again on last year's weeds, skimmed on the surface of the water. I walked up and down hummocks, stumbled on lumps and bumps. Finally, a flock of yellowlegs, the shorebirds that I had been waiting for. That lesser legs was barely visible in this landscape, I had to stop and search for it feeding just fifteen metres away. A common loon flew overhead into the north. There, a V of thirteen cormorants, a Wilson's phalarope, a willet called, a black-crowned night heron in the sky. Here, a savannah sparrow perched on a stalk of dried grass beside me carolled its song to the world. I watched a group of shovellers, male and female, drake and hen, two of each. They bobbed their heads and grunted. They bobbled and pumped and preened, dabbled. They flew up, and darted, and chased each other. Little pockmarks on the water, it wanted to rain again.

That millions-of-years-old cycle: mating, breeding, nesting, raising young. Animal, vegetable, all living organisms. That quartet of shovellers. Their annual ritual, their avian *soirée*. Watch how that blue-winged teal drake stutters and bends, how he beaks and bows for his mate. I remember how we used to strut the high-school halls in the hope of a female audience; I see it in Jon now, with his friends, the brag and bravado. Earth's extravagance, indulgence, in giving life, in taking it. Mating, breeding, the substance of bird behaviour; millions of bird young born each year, so few of them will survive the first winter. That mink I saw earlier with a red-winged blackbird clasped and twitching in its mouth; nature's bloody lap.

I watched a palm warbler flutter and fly in a bit of brush, an upland sandpiper teeter on a fence post. He bobbed his pigeon head while his mate wandered through the pasture. I leaned against a post along the way, I watched and waited. Sometimes it pays to stand and wait. Here, suddenly, not three metres away, I had flushed a sora, a kind of secretive marsh hen. Yellow bill. Black mask and throat. Grey cheeks, brown cap. Distinct and brilliant markings on its back, its tail. What a gorgeous creature. My first sighting of a sora wasn't really a sighting at all. Susan and I had stopped beside a slough east of Boissevain in southern Manitoba to name the several species of duck we saw there: blue-winged teal, mallard, northern shoveller. We heard a sora whinny, I recognized the sound from tapes and TV shows. When you see a sora, often it's at the edge of a patch of marsh grass; you catch a flash, a movement, and then it's gone, you wonder if you saw anything at all. This sora lifted its leg and stepped, it poked with its bill in the water, it pumped its tail, it wandered around at my feet in the meadow as if I weren't even there, as if I were nobody, as if I were a cattail. I watched for maybe five minutes, maybe thirty minutes. How can you tell time if you're pretending to be a cattail?

Civilizations have always come and gone, the Roman, the Mayan, the Chinese. Somewhere species have been born, have grown to extinction. Children come, grandparents leave again. I wonder sometimes why I feel so much pleasure in the passing of geese and ducks in the sky, in the migration of shorebirds, in the long slow loop of an eagle, the call of a sora. I think how they judge their own rhythms, their mate's splendour, the curve of each season. The earth in the morning feels alive and exquisite and changing, must have for millions of years already, might for a million years yet. Geese still have hope for that future. The marsh weaves a promise for them, dried grass and pond, offers a home, wakens a rush of desire. Ducks still fly and breed, and fly and breed again. Songbirds call, warble their dream of mates and eggs, birth and migration. They sing in the face of their fear, their death and extinction. When the geese pass in the sky in fall and in spring, I always wish I could fly along.

I drove past the fences and fields and deeper into the marsh. I stopped near the water, wide and open water. The ruddy ducks dove. Redheads flew up in pairs and around. That Canada goose on the ridge, there, surrounded by water, motionless, already nesting. I caught a patch of white, a great egret, sheltered in the reeds and cattails. The egret preened and waited, preened and waited. It humped its back, turned its head from left to right to left again. A pair of gadwalls drifted by. A northern shoveller. A ring-necked duck, black head and crown erect, sharp white trim on his bill. I was surprised the other day when Susan asked if I'd noticed that the ring-necked duck actually had a bit of brown collar. "Did you ever see that?" she said. I didn't want to answer. And a mallard. That mallard would be done with mating soon enough. Once the eggs were fertilized and laid he'd fly with all the other mallard drakes into the middle of the marsh to moult. A black tern flapped and wheeled above the surface of the pond, it flapped and wheeled and dove.

I watched the egret again, I thought it might do something. I was hoping it would do something; maybe catch a fish, or fly, find another egret, its mate. I was watching for a signal. The egret preened and waited. It turned its head, ruffled its feathers. I watched for fifteen minutes, for twenty minutes. Would the egret nest here in the marsh? I watched for forty-five minutes. No need for the egret to fly if there was no danger, to feed if it wasn't hungry. The egret waited. I began to think of it as a patient bird, all this waiting. But my picture of the egret was all wrong, I was the one waiting. The egret crouched deeper among the reeds. I watched for sixty minutes. One hour. I felt surprised how long an hour lasted, waiting in the marsh for an egret to move. I noticed a grebe to my right, horned, I think. I lifted my binoculars to see, the grebe dove, was gone. I saw another grebe, I lifted my binoculars again, gone. They seemed to arch their necks, jump and dive in one motion, they were gone for a while, and up again. Coots cackled and cooed in the rushes; a spotted sandpiper stuttered across the water, landed to bob on a rock nearby. A skunk ambled down the trail to the east.

I heard the drone of an airplane, my great egret lifted its head, it turned, I saw long feathers trailing from its back. Some species of egret were hunted almost to extinction at the turn of the century, those breeding plumes taken as decoration for women's hats. I thought I could get a better look at those feathers, those plumes. I took one step. Another. And a third. Too many. Suddenly, a chorus started over the water. The ducks and the terns in the marsh called their alarm. The grebes dove again, the coots rushed for cover. The egret saw itself exposed. It flew, as if from a memory of that terrible hundred-year-old hunt, it flew farther and farther into the marsh. Its flight, my signal; not the one I wanted. I had dared to step closer, too close, I had somehow bumped across a boundary. Frightened, the egret had flown with its headdress deep into the marsh.

Short-eared owl

Talk About the Future

Burrowing owls still nest in Manitoba, though the roost is growing thin; in 1995 only four nesting pairs were reported, by now those too will probably be gone. Birdwatchers sometimes talk about their personal jinx birds, birds they never seem to see, even if some impassioned companion birder "saw it here just a minute ago." This small owl—Billy owl, *la chouette à terrier*—has offered its own kind of grail for me; Susan and I have made five or six trips over the last five years to a far corner of the province to see it. We like to see owls anyway, they hold a compelling attraction, and we've heard how comical the burrowing owl looks standing on the ground on its long legs at the mouth of a nest hole, how it stares back at you; we'd like to mark it on our Manitoba checklist before it disappears. We've worked from a book, *Birder's Guide to Southwestern Manitoba*, from reports of other bird enthusiasts, the notes of wildlife officers. Pipestone, Pierson, Goodlands, Broomhill, Dalny, Tilston, Hartney, Medora, Lauder, Underhill, Deloraine. We've driven up and down gravel roads, risked ruts and mud roads, weathered storms and heat and insects, headaches, exhaustion. We've turned left, turned right, left again, right; stopped beside badlands and fenced pasture. We've watched and waited, we've scanned and scoped, rested to the song of calling cattle. We've tried to persuade Richardson's ground squirrels into new and owl-like shapes, to cajole the tops of fence posts into *coo-cooing* or flying. We have found other birds; our first loggerhead shrike in a string of poplars just west of Coulter, a pair of ferruginous hawks in a cottonwood along the Souris River, a great crested flycatcher in Lyleton, eastern and mountain bluebirds on fence and hydro wires, stilt sandpipers, catbirds and thrashers, chestnut-collared longspurs, a Say's phoebe outside a deserted farmhouse west of Napinka. Each trip ended in disappointment, we couldn't find any burrowing owls. Susan, I think, sometimes wished we would stop looking altogether; "Let's just forget about them."

If you drive west along the Trans-Canada Highway from Winnipeg in early June the prairie stands fresh and green and open. You notice the horizon, how far it is. Giant fields of grain reaching for their summer clothes, miles and miles, there, finally touch the sky. Clusters of trees and brush dot the landscape, farmyards, shelter belts, maybe the odd pond. You'll delight at the beauty in modern farm practice, these large-scale farming operations. You'll wonder how anything can be this simple; one big sky, one expanse of growing grain; one colour green, one blue, nothing else. I picked Susan up at work on a bright and sultry Friday afternoon. We had packed a few things the night before—extra clothes, food and drink, repellent—for our drive to Melita, Manitoba, another burrowing owl excursion. We had all our fingers crossed. We hoped to find a spot with eight or nine young birds, some wild, others recently released; this time we had foolproof owl directions, we felt we needed them.

We drove that stretch of the Trans-Canada, farms, straight and open fields, the horizon. My father, if he'd been along, would have told us the story of each quarter section:

wheat or flax, what it was, early or late, whether it needed rain. He would have told us again of the horse-drawn grain wagons he built in his shop in Niverville in 1945; of his favourite horse, a grey named Fanny; of all the wild ones he shod during the war in the lumber camp; his stories would have drifted even farther to the past, childhood in Ukraine. He would have compared the scenery; "These last five miles look almost like the road from Molotchna."

At MacGregor we noticed that everything seemed to get suddenly brushier, fields now curving round the edge of bush, more fence posts and pastures; maybe the farms weren't quite as well-to-do. We caught a dark green ridge rising to the south, Carberry Hills, the Spruce Woods Provincial Forest, once temporary home to naturalist Ernest Thompson Seton. A jackrabbit bounded across an empty meadow. The temperature at four p.m. was somewhere in the low thirties; we'd passed large pieces of rubber lying on the highway, truck tires, I imagined them exploding in the heat. Then, near Austin, the road began to dip and roll and sway, a road sign announced *Deer Crossing*. No stretch of grain here, only forest, and cattle, a beautiful wild country, rolling hills and willows, bur oak and pine. I said to Susan that someday I'd like to live here, perched on one of these gentle hills, a house with windows all around; my father likes the grain, I fancy the wild country. Susan pointed to a picture of a ruffed grouse at the side of the road, the Wildlands Conservation Project. Above the grouse sign a red-tailed hawk circled the sky, crows chased and plunged and played in the wind.

The prairie swept on and on. Douglas Marsh, Brandon, the Assiniboine River valley; somewhere we'd crossed a perimeter, now that long green ridge of hills rose to the north. At the town of Griswold we turned south and the province seemed to fall away in front of us. We passed a herd of longhorn cattle. Every quarter section of land now offered its own marsh or slough. Driving on the Trans-Canada we'd seen robins and goldfinches, western and eastern kingbirds, barn, cliff and tree swallows, kestrels, meadowlarks, killdeers, savannah and chipping sparrows, Brewer's and red-winged blackbirds. South of Griswold, we counted waterfowl: redhead and scaup and canvasback; mallard, teal and shoveller; pied-billed grebe and coot. We passed willets and yellowlegs, upland sandpipers, great blue herons, ring-billed and Franklin's gulls, Forster's and black terns, common snipe. The landscape changed from farmland to slough, from bush to slough to farmland.

Four-hour drive from Winnipeg to Melita—when we noticed the elevator rising against the sky we checked our instructions. We slipped through town, found the landmarks we'd jotted on a piece of paper and made the first turn right. Our excitement grew, we thought this time we'd surely find our burrowing owl. We followed a dogleg left, right, left. We drove eight miles and turned right. We drove six miles and turned right again. Another half mile and we stopped in the middle of a field of alfalfa. We knew there was a storm coming, had seen the clouds gathering in the west. We'd heard the warning on the radio—heavy rain, hail, intense wind. What does it take to see a *foolproof* burrowing owl? One minute? Less. Thirty, twenty seconds? The thunderstorm hit just as we pulled the telescope out of our pack. The sky rumbled and flashed, the wind whistled, raindrops popped against our windshield. We scoped for a minute or two, no owls. We thought we had little choice, we couldn't risk sitting out here on the naked prairie in a storm. We might get stuck, we might get hit by lightning, our Honda Civic wasn't built for this kind of adventure. We turned, drove the eight miles of mud and gravel road back to the highway and Melita. Maybe we could come back early tomorrow, maybe the roads would be okay by morning, maybe the owls would wait until morning; I felt sick with disappointment.

The burrowing owl has been in decline in Canada since the mid-1950s. The twenty-three nesting pairs reported in Manitoba in 1993 had turned to four nesting pairs in 1995.

Authorities report that the decline is almost certainly due to intensified land use. Twentieth-century human habits make life difficult for birds, the burrowing owl is losing its battle with modern agriculture; large-scale farming operations. Farmers continue to seed more and more waste and pasture land to grain. The agricultural pesticide carbofuran kills not only the burrowing owls' staple prey—grasshoppers—it kills the burrowing owl as well. Until a few weeks ago, in my naïveté, I was convinced that I would someday have to become a vegetarian, I owed it to my children, to the future and the environment. Now, I'm not so sure. Burrowing owls seem to favour nesting on land regularly grazed by cattle— waste and pasture land again; the grass stays short, parent owls can watch for predators. Maybe if we all ate more steak and hamburger, if we spun grain fields back to cattle and pasture, maybe we could save the burrowing owl in Manitoba. I wish solutions were that simple.

The whooping crane may never have been abundant in North America, estimates suggest about 1,400 birds in the mid-1800s. Still, Ernest Thompson Seton, in *The Birds of Manitoba*, 1891, tells us that the whooping crane was once a fairly common migrant in the Souris River country, that it could be seen near Winnipeg in summer. Biologists agree that it once nested in Manitoba. But with the conversion of wetland and prairie to grain and hay production, with increased crane hunting, both for meat and feathers, by 1940 the North American whooping crane population had fallen below twenty birds. Human disturbance, the major factor. More whooping cranes continue to die from collisions with power lines than from any other known cause. Others are killed by hunters who claim to mistake them for sandhill cranes. Conservationists have struggled for this half-century to bring the population back to its current total of approximately fifty nesting pairs. Whooping cranes continue to be seen in Manitoba; near Churchill in 1953, near Gillam in 1974. In late April 1996, three separate sightings were reported in the vicinity of Oak Hammock Marsh.

Three sightings, enough to raise the enthusiasm of any local naturalist; maybe one day the whooping crane will nest again in Manitoba.

You may question the nature of late spring storms on the prairie—"nothing to worry about." But if you live there, you know how destructive they can be, always strong winds and the chance of a tornado. By the time Susan and I returned to Melita the rain had stopped, the clouds had drifted dark into

Eastern kingbird

the northeast, we still had a long hour of sunlight left, must have just caught the edge of that storm. We stopped to fill our gas tank, booked into a motel, and started back on our route—supper would have to wait. Had we found the right spot? We checked our landmarks again. Eight miles, six miles, left, right, right. We stopped again on our mud trail through the alfalfa and surveyed the south pasture, the sun shone bright on the west horizon.

It was one of those evenings after a storm when your eyes seem to open a bit wider, you sense some kind of hidden surprise. The air felt fresh and cool after the heat of the afternoon, rain still sparkled on the grass. You caught the colours of the pasture, of the bales of rolled hay, of each individual fence post, a grey and crumbling building. You noticed texture, shapes, edges crisp and well-defined. Western kingbirds called and fluttered above the barbed wire. A vesper sparrow hopped along the trail in front of the car. Blackbirds—red-winged—flocked round an oak and a great horned owl. You understood for a moment that tonight your skin somehow didn't quite contain you, that your boundaries had failed. Suddenly a brown spot on a post in the pasture. There, another. Telescope, binoculars, Susan and I watched and wondered. Burrowing owls perched and bobbed and hovered, they chattered and *cohooed*, they swivelled their round owl heads, five, six of them. I left Susan with the telescope and wandered east down the trail. More birds. A sharp-tailed grouse feeding beside a cluster of hay bales. Warbling vireo, clay-coloured sparrow, and a catbird calling from an acre of poplar and box elder. Baird's sparrows whistled and trilled in the alfalfa. A ferruginous hawk cried in the sky above us.

Burrowing owl, whooping crane; you wonder how long these species will survive. Piping plovers seem to flirt with extinction, the nests I saw this year in Manitoba so close to the water's edge the slightest wind or rise in water levels I'm sure would have drowned them. Records show that double-crested cormorants were slaughtered in huge numbers in

Manitoba as far back as 1927. And the slaughter continues. Fishermen on Lake Winnipegosis estimate that they destroyed forty thousand cormorant nests last year. They know it's against the law. They believe that colonial water birds—double-crested cormorants, American white pelicans—are responsible for the decline in commercial fish stocks; they forget that fish and bird have lived in balance for thousands of years, long before the birth of our commercial fishery. Naturalists report that when these angry fishermen appear with their flame throwers and guns and clubs on the rocky reefs and islands of Winnipegosis they destroy everything: pelican, gull, tern and cormorant. Both cormorant and pelican populations, having just recovered from the DDT of the '50s and '60s, now face renewed threats. I prefer more pleasant stories.

Four o'clock in the morning and the northeastern sky already begins to pale. A house finch moves in the cluster of box elder and elm behind my backyard feeder, the neighbourhood whispers with birdsong. I look at my watch again; June 21, I hadn't intended that, it's the first day of summer. I adjust myself in the car, fasten my seatbelt. I thought I was getting up early enough, I wanted to visit Oak Hammock Marsh at sunrise, need to hurry now to get there. I saw my first house finch in Winnipeg in 1993. In April 1995, a breeding pair collected nesting material in my backyard and flew into the blue spruce in front of the house. What a lot of excitement. I called my birding friends, they came over to see, house finches nesting in Manitoba, we watched and talked and pointed. A windstorm destroyed that nest, but by early summer six of those finches fed regularly at my feeder. Shipped illegally from the southwest and released on Long Island, New York, in the early 1940s, the house finch, with its rich and warbling song, has now spread throughout most of the United States and into southern Canada—spread so quickly that in some areas it outnumbers the house sparrow. Mountain bluebirds—thanks to the bluebird trail, all those bluebird nest boxes nailed to posts along back-country roads—seem to be making a return. Susan and I, on our hawk and burrowing owl trips, often catch their phantom blues and greys on fence posts or wires in southern Manitoba. Though thousands are still killed each year in North America because of their perceived threat to livestock, the coyote, once a western species, has pushed its range north and east and south into most of North and Central America; it even thrives in our cities. The wily coyote—it can sing its song outside my window any day; legend holds that it will be the last creature to survive.

At sunrise the marsh already bustles with life. Terns hover and spin, ducks preen and feed, horned grebes dive, blackbirds chase along the edge of the water. Common yellowthroats call from the cattails. The first flock of cormorants flaps high above me in the sky. And a pair of marbled godwits—large shorebirds, long bills extended and cinnamon wings, *terwhiit, terwhiit, terwhiit*—flies low again in the direction of the pasture where I found them nesting last year. Song sparrow, marsh wren, sora, savannah sparrow, I point my microcassette, I'll hear them all again later at my desk. These eastern kingbirds fidget and sputter, we've come too close to their nest. Daring birds, they'll attack any hawk or raven or crow that comes this close, they've even been seen to attack a low-flying airplane. The grass along the marsh side of the trail stretches tall and green, the prairie falls away on the other, maybe a sedge wren in the ditches to our right. Pintail, green-winged teal, redhead, scaup, black-crowned night heron; they fly up around us on our walk, alarmed to see us in the marsh this early, to see us in the marsh at all.

I've brought a companion for the morning walk today; Jon, I picked him up at his mom's house, it was early. He read to me in the car as we drove, a short story about horses, about fathers and sons, about some cruelty. He must have planned this; he crawled into the car, he got out his book and began to read. His voice rang strong and clear:

> *Following his father's death, Joseph Kelsey*
> *discovered, in his bereavement, a passion for*
> *horses. Joseph's passion for horses was not of*
> *the same character as the old man's had been;*
> *Joseph's was searching, secretive, concerned*
> *with lore, confined to books. It was not love . . .*
> (Guy Vanderhaeghe, *A Man on Horseback*)

I couldn't help but wonder about this reading, the bed-time story twice displaced. Now, on the trail, he catches me by surprise again, asks whether the story reminds me of my father. I thought it probably reminded him of me; fathers, and cruelty, our good, our poisoned sides.

We talk, my son and I. He tells me about the distribution of wealth. "So much of the world's wealth," he says, "is held by so few people." He says he might someday work for the New Democratic Party. He talks about Nietzsche and nihilism, about international development, about the history of science, about the sun, the moon, the stars; all his university subjects. Exciting. He discusses the possibilities of his future—an education, marriage, a daughter, a son. I listen. He pokes fun at the notes I speak onto my cassette; I don't mind, sons are meant to sometimes tease their fathers. Then I tell him about northern harriers, about long-billed dowitchers, yellowlegs—lesser and greater—about the American bittern that flashes up suddenly at our feet. "See the brown flight feathers, the streaking on the neck and breast." Jon says he saw a great blue heron nest last summer while canoeing in Turtle Mountain Provincial Park, actually saw its three olive eggs. I tell him he's lucky to have seen a heron nest, I wish I'd seen it; tell him that I've seen a hummingbird nest, that was lucky too. He says, "I guess we're even, Dad."

The clear sky of this morning's drive has turned to cloud, and wind, light drizzle. A muskrat raises its head on the trail in front of us. "Muskrat," Jon speaks again, and smiles. I look at him, catch the invitation in his eye; we laugh, and dash toward it. The muskrat, far too quick for us, doesn't even seem to run, just vanishes. We try again to flush a marsh wren for a better look. Here's one rustling and rattling in the cattails. We catch a blur before it disappears again, hides low in the marsh; two metres away and we can't see it. Other marsh wrens bubble up nearby, they seem to nest in colonies. There, we've frightened a savannah sparrow out of the grass, it flutters and runs along the trail before us. When we stop, it stops. We look for a nest; should be here somewhere, better not step on it. We search, we watch, we wait; maybe this sparrow will lead us in another direction, give us some other clue to the future.

How quickly things change in the marsh, one visit to the next, constant change. Mallard and shoveller drakes, after the ritual and dance of last month's mating, have now become shy. They look ragged and dirty, have begun their moult, begun to shed their old feathers and replace them with new ones, won't be able to fly for a few weeks. The hens keep busy with their young, hatching or feeding, watching for danger, they will moult later. This mallard hen, when she sees us, flaps and splashes, pretends she's injured and struggling in the water, hopes her eight ducklings will swim away undetected. That mallard bursts suddenly from a patch of alfalfa, leaves her nest of eleven eggs. Blue-winged teal and ruddy ducks aren't as far into their cycle, still hold their mating colours. And those three buffleheads, what are they doing here this late in the season? Those two wool-headed drakes still strut for their hen, no moulting for them. Diving ducks, buffleheads usually nest in stumps and hollow trees, I thought they would breed on forest lakes; I see only one tree here at the south tip of this pond, perhaps they've found a wood-duck box that suits them.

Change. A fast trail this morning, because of the rain, because of the young legs beside me. And real conversation, less attention paid to the marsh markers as they pass. Change. Jon, the child of yesterday, suddenly adult, must have happened in India. On the last stretch of the trail a killdeer calls an alarm. It flutters, flops, calls and calls. It shakes its wings, fans its tail, calls. It runs and calls at our feet, works so hard for our attention. We stop, look around, we're afraid we might step on its eggs, must be very close to a nest. There—I catch my breath—I see them, four eggs, pale greenish brown and speckled with black, pointed in and down at the centre. Four eggs on a bed of pebbles, I can hardly breathe to see them. Silverweed—green jagged leaves, small yellow flowers, red runners, my finger still clicks on the microcassette—grows all around them. Two metres away the poor killdeer, even more concerned now that we're bending over the nest, still sprawls and flutters, flops and calls, fans its tail, looks at us with its red eyes, wonders why its ruse doesn't work. It comes running at us, calls, sprawls again. Sometimes when I get home and listen to my notes on the cassette I'm surprised what else I hear, despair in the throat of the killdeer.

Birds have unwrapped an enchanting world for me, their colour, their habits, their migration, their adaptations. One bird easily leads to another, one dozen species to one hundred. Unfamiliar places, unusual books, new stories and friends, a bagful of bird surprises. Like Jon, at the beginning of his adult life, I too feel my world opening before me. Sunrise . . . The killdeer, *Charadrius vociferus* (it is), knows nothing of the trouble that faces burrowing owl, whooping crane, piping plover populations; knows nothing of the slaughter of the cormorant, though I wonder whether killdeer young die too on those Winnipegosis islands. Common to rural areas and open city spaces, killdeers nest from southern Canada to northern Chile. I've known the killdeer all my life, known its call, it used to follow us around when we harrowed an open field in southern Ontario, my dad and I on the tractor, it ran and called and dabbled. The killdeer lives from year to year, moves simply with the seasons, knows what to eat, where to fly. It will try anything to save its nest, drag its wing and shriek to distract a dog, fly in the face of a horse. The killdeer is desperate to save its eggs, it will gladly risk the horse, the coyote or dog, knows it needs somehow to save its young and its nest.

A passion for horses. When Jon turned four he carried a book, he memorized the breeds of horses: Arabian, Thoroughbred, Percheron, Morgan, Hackney, names I knew and understood. Parent, child, grandchild, the messages they send to one another, within or across the genders. Here on the trail beyond the killdeer nest a horse hoofprint, five inches across. Jon and I stoop again, run our fingers along its rim.

Upland sandpiper

Bur Oak and Coulee

Wouldn't you sometimes just like to know what people think of you, how you look in other people's eyes? You imagine over a coffee, or a glass of wine, on a moonlit night that it would bolster your self-confidence, make you feel better about yourself; it could give you a whole new perspective, turn your life around. You think it might surprise you. I was shocked a few months ago to read in the *Winnipeg Sun* that I had been unlucky in love. Had they sent some reporter down to follow me, watch from my bedroom closet? How could the *Sun* have discovered that about me? The writer went on to talk about a collection of short stories that I had written, sad and funny love stories—friends of mine, you understand—she thought they must be a mirror for my life. Love has brought turmoil, and adventures, but not at all sad ones for me; maybe that writer was too preoccupied with her own misfortunes. Still, her reading gave me a jerk, a kind of intestinal rope burn, didn't last much longer than a day.

When my father and mother married in 1931 they

settled for a few years in a small town called Enterprise in southwestern Manitoba. They bought a house about the size of my living room, they raised their first children, entertained friends and family there—I remember the stories; Grandma, Grandpa, Uncle and Aunt, all those people sleeping for the weekend in one small house. Love and adventure! My father opened his first blacksmith shop. The customers paid him in eggs and milk and sausages, never on time, his customers had no money, nobody had any money, but eventually they brought him something. My parents survived Enterprise, though they lost their oldest daughter there, she'd barely learned to walk and talk. In August 1992, now eighty-three years old, my father came to visit from Ontario. He came with a plan, he wanted to drive out to Enterprise, make a day of it, he said he'd had a dream. He dreamt that he had found the wedding ring Mom had lost so many years ago while working as a newlywed in the vegetable garden. My mother had died in 1983, I guess he wished to recapture something of their life and youth together.

He knew exactly where the village had stood on Highway #3, though there was nothing left of it; I saw only the highway, a mile road, a coulee, some bur oak and willow. And farmland, crops—wheat, barley, canola, sunflower—miles and miles of farmland. My father showed us, three of us standing beside him, my sister and brother-in-law. "There," he said. "The elevator. The train track. The store. Our house. Our well. And the blacksmith shop." A handful of memories and a huge blue sky. My father looked around, he paced here and there, turned to face the oak and the coulee. He pointed: "This is where our garden used to be, here's where Mom lost her ring." I think my father saw then the nature of his journey; we were all faced twelve metres into the middle of a wheat field, metre-high wheat, and dense. He took a few steps into the field, he kicked at the sod with his black shoes. "Well," he said, "I guess I won't ever find that ring here. How many times do you think this field has been tilled since we had our vegetable garden here? Or ploughed even." We three didn't say anything. "I don't know if I thought I would find the ring hanging from a stalk of wheat," he said. Almost humour. We all looked out over the field a while longer. We got in the car and began our drive back to Winnipeg. "I always felt lucky your mom married me," my father said. "All my life I felt lucky"; he shook his head and turned to look at me.

No ring, but maybe my dad found something in that field in Enterprise, some other thought or image, maybe we never find exactly the things we look for. I don't know what I'm looking for, where I'm going—never did, all the way back to high school—what I should do with my life, what thread I'm following. Maybe that's my luck, I don't know, I made it this far. I do get tired sometimes of putting words on a screen, on paper. Do words still matter these days? Words on paper? Does anybody read them? We're all too busy sleeping in front of the TV. Sometimes I'm still tempted to think in old absolutes, black and white. Either there is a God, or there isn't. Either I have three million readers, or I have none. Either I know exactly where I'm going, or if I don't, I've been lost for a lifetime. Nothing in between.

I went out boating a few weeks ago with some friends near Willow Island, we wanted to see some birds before breakfast. At the farthest point on our journey the boat motor suddenly wouldn't work, clutch, I think. We realized we'd have to paddle across a large lagoon to get home. So we paddled. While the wind howled. Two-foot waves rocked the boat over and over, we hoped we could beach on that far shore. We didn't know if we might wash out into Lake Winnipeg, if we would capsize and drown; that would have been tragedy for us. Maybe I'm blowing the story out of proportion, I'm not that crazy about water. Whether we'd make it across the lagoon, survive, drink a cup of strong coffee, eat waffles for breakfast. Waffles would be rhapsody. You see what I mean about absolutes. We didn't drown, we had a good breakfast, three hours late, but that afternoon I felt unhappy again; I should have thrilled to still be alive. There are some things I know. About love. I've never doubted it, the feeling; I love those bur oak and willow coulees. About direction? I do know one thing, right now I'm in the car and driving in the direction of Oak Hammock Marsh.

The mosquito knows its purpose, that's how it seems; to buzz, to bite me, to gather blood, to lay eggs so there will be more mosquitoes to bite me. There are over three thousand mosquito species in the world, at least seventy-four of those in Canada. The females are the ones that take your blood, they take three times their body weight in blood, they need to feed on mammal blood at least once before their eggs will develop properly; the males eat only fruit and plant juices. In summer the mosquito life cycle takes only two or three weeks to complete, but eggs can lie dormant for many months and some Canadian species overwinter as adults and live for as long as nine months. In the northern forests mosquito bites can result in serious blood loss for animals. We've been told that purple martins eat two thousand mosquitoes a day, apparently that's not true. But martins, and other swallows, flycatchers, probably some warblers, even dragonflies, do eat adult mosquitoes. (The eastern kingbird, a flycatcher, eats more than two hundred different kinds of insects, and the fruit or seeds of forty different plants.) And small fish and aquatic insects eat mosquito larvae in large quantities.

I'm not that excited about visiting the marsh today, I wonder about mosquitoes, I expect the mosquitoes will be terrible, I think the flycatchers and swallows haven't been doing their job. Growing up at home in southern Ontario we saw very few mosquitoes, and I was horrified on my first trip to Manitoba to get out of the car at dusk and notice the hordes of mosquitoes descending on my face and arms. Mosquitoes are very clear about their purpose. I've read somewhere that caribou on the tundra will sometimes be driven mad by the swarming of insects. I think I understood the caribou's desperation that first evening in Manitoba, I felt a panic at being swarmed by that cloud of mosquitoes, I wanted to run. I should be okay today though, I've brought all my mosquito equipment: a mild insect lotion, a small bottle of DEET, pale clothes, a mosquito shirt and hat.

I slow the car for a traffic light. A flock of small birds, warblers I think, eight or ten of them, skips across the sky just above tree level. Hard to imagine that for them fall migration has begun already. Olive, grey, green, yellow, orange, red, blue, chestnut, black and white, warbler migration is one of the most colourful and exciting of North American bird occasions. Warblers flit from branch to branch, tree to tree, everywhere on your block, searching leaves and limbs for insects, so busy, so very hard to fix them in the eyepiece of your binoculars. As the traffic light changes I see four more warblers. The falcon, when it comes, comes from below. Sweeps up. Flops back and forth, from wing to wing. Twists. Flops again. Fans its wing and tail feathers, picks a warbler from the sky. Several years ago Susan and I invited people for a barbecue in our backyard on Ashburn Street, fifteen or twenty people, we drank punch and visited on the deck while I tended the fire and the meat. I looked up for a moment that day, mid-sentence—a blue Winnipeg evening sky—and a female merlin appeared in the open air three metres above me. Appeared, caught a chipping sparrow, and was gone. Not a sound. I looked around me, nothing, nobody else had noticed, I couldn't believe it. That's probably how most living beings die, without much warning or announcement. My oldest sister in Enterprise, how often do we think of her now?

I watch the way the mist rises from the water in creeks and drainage ditches. I see combines on the side roads. See cars hurrying their drivers off to work, a killdeer legging across the highway. A cold morning today, six degrees, the promise of frost to come soon. A pair of western kingbirds perches on a hydro wire along Highway 8. My friend John calls them Arkansas kingbirds, he says he remembers them from his childhood, everybody called them that, he never heard the name *western kingbird* before I told him. My 1945 Taverner's *Birds of Canada* lists an Arkansas kingbird, "western kingbird" beside it in smaller letters. But the map in National Geographic's *Field Guide to the Birds of North America* doesn't even place Arkansas in the western kingbird's nesting range. Arkansas kingbird, I wonder about the origin of that name. How far does that go back? Should be a book somewhere about the origin of bird names.

Already the blackbirds flock in hundreds, they swing from field to field. Here, the hydro wires heavy and sagging with blackbirds along the road. Three, four hundred blackbirds, I drive up beside them and count. Most of them Brewer's blackbirds, and a few red-wings. There, a yellow-headed blackbird in the group. Two, three more. And swallows swirling in the sky over a dusty blue barn. Barn swallows, their long forked tails, and a few tree swallows, they're chasing insects. One of these mornings soon those swallows will all be gone. Cattails cluster along the road. Sow thistle. Western dock. The mist rises from a creek to cloak both wood duck and mallard. A song sparrow sings from the marsh grasses. Somewhere a yellowlegs calls. A savannah sparrow chips and grooms in a stand of narrow-leaved sunflower. Savannah by the yellow lore, white eyebrow, it's so busy stretching and turning to preen that I can see the pink of its skin beneath the feathers. And sun. And sun. And sun. A summer of sun, most beautiful summer this year.

I think back over my first writing visits to the marsh. What were my reasons for going? What was I looking for? What did I discover? I managed to escape the desk and the blank page—for a few days—though I found these words much harder to write than I'd expected. I found a few trees, a few flowers. Names. I discovered names, and what they stood for: cottonwood, box elder, bur oak, red-osier dogwood, yellow wood sorrel, white sweet-clover, western dock, red samphire, silverweed, many-flowered aster. Mink:

a dark brown body, white under the chin, black tail, legs so short that its belly often leaves a furrow in the snow. I discovered the Arkansas kingbird. Books and pages full of names.

A pasture along the highway, horses, a dark dappled roan with his member hanging almost to the ground; and suddenly I think about sex. Sex. I've almost missed the sex implicit in these Oak Hammock sketches. Birds, insects, vegetation, birth, growth, death, everything here is about sex, reproduction, keeping the genes alive. The mating of ducks in spring, just the sight of them, I never mentioned how that woke me, how my blood and my imagination boiled. Odd I wouldn't have shouted something, a woman's name, maybe someone from high school. Angela! The beauty every boy desired. What other feelings have I ignored? What process of editing did I employ? How have I chosen to write about one thought and not another? Why did I leave out all the *bloody*s and *damn*s that are a part of everyday language? Why didn't I mention the McDonald's this morning, how angry I got when they couldn't serve my egg and biscuit at six-thirty the way I'd expected?

A Forster's tern wheels above a pond. White below, pale grey above, black cap, red-orange bill. I learned, much to my chagrin earlier this year, that I've probably been mistaking terns for the last seven years; I don't know what to do now with my birding records. The most prevalent tern in southern Manitoba is, in fact, not the common tern but Forster's tern. I've been studying their respective descriptions and calls, have become reluctant to name either one. A group of thirty yellowlegs flashes by, yellowlegs used to be that way for me, lesser or greater. This sandpiper they leave behind should be easier to name than the tern. Such a beautiful look through my scope, all the markings so fresh and clear. Strong white eyebrow. Black legs and bill. Scalloped back, pale grey breast band, white throat, clear white belly. Semipalmated sandpiper. It steps back and forth, lifts its wings for balance, picks at the surface of the water. Named for the webbing between its front toes, the semipalmated sandpiper nests on the northern shores of Canada and Alaska, winters in South America; its migration, too, has begun. A black tern passes just beyond the sandpiper. And higher in the sky, against the sun, a falcon harasses a buteo.

At 8:20 I leave the Oak Hammock parking lot. I pass bank swallows, goldfinches, yellow warblers, a yellow-shafted flicker in the willow bluff. Since the publication of Roger Tory Peterson's field guides, birders have come to speak of *confusing fall warblers*. In late summer and fall, with moulting and juvenile plumage, many of North America's forty warbler species begin to look very much alike. This confusing warbler here—yellow throat, breast and belly, olive green above, no wing bars, slight eye-ring—is probably a Nashville warbler. That sparrow on the wooden railing shows a dark central breast spot and a strong stripe bordering its white throat, a song sparrow. Two fledglings, much bigger than the parent, chase it from perch to perch, they want to be fed. That song sparrow, I think, may have been duped by some brown-headed cowbird, may be raising two cowbird young. The cowbird, sometimes also called cuckold or lazy bird, is one of several North American brood parasites. Cowbird females lay all their eggs in the nests of other species of birds which then hatch the eggs and raise the young as though they were their own. Several species of cuckoo and grebe, even roadrunners and brown thrashers, practise brood parasitism to a lesser degree; they usually raise their own young but also lay eggs in the nests of other kinds of birds. A clay-coloured sparrow calls in a willow, and a common yellowthroat. There, the falcon again, a big one, peregrine I'm sure.

I walk beyond the willows where a blue-winged teal mother quacks and leads her young across the water away from me. Mid-August, these eight young still look quite downy and yellow, as though they weren't born that long ago; must have been a late nest, maybe the first one failed. The drake, like most male ducks, has left his young family, probably before they hatched, flown off somewhere to moult with other blue-winged males. Blue-winged teal arrive late on the prairies anyway, they have a long way to fly, they winter in Central and South America. One bird banded in Saskatchewan was recorded later in the same year eleven thousand kilometres away in Peru. That young coot at the water's edge stands as tall as its parents, has lost all trace of the reddish down that veiled its tiny head and shoulders a few weeks ago. And the pied-billed grebe young, they still show their zigzag facial markings, though they look full-grown—far too big now to rest on their fathers' backs—and their parents have deserted them. Deserted, did you notice that word? Their parents have *deserted* them. The blue-winged teal drake has *left* his young family. Cowbird, *lazy* bird. Do you notice how we often want to judge birds by human standards?

Grebes, I've discovered, eat their own feathers; nobody seems to know why. One pied-billed grebe stomach studied in 1962 was more than half filled with feathers. Grebes also eat fish, crayfish, snails, frogs, the seeds of aquatic plants, a variety of insects—including the nymphs of dragonflies. I have seen far more dragonflies this year in Winnipeg than ever before, swarms of them in spring at Fisher Park just two blocks from my home. And fishflies too, some mornings in July the east windows on Osborne Street shops shook and shimmered with fishflies. Maybe these marsh studies have made me more aware, maybe I just never noticed these things before. Or maybe they came with this year's flood, the Big Flood, the one that rose higher than 1950. Lots of water, lots of dragon- and fishflies. The black flies in Winnipeg earlier this year apparently *were* a result of the flood, they bit me while I mowed the lawn, my arms turned hot and red and lumpy. Here, two kilometres into the marsh, my eyes follow dragonflies, black bodies with neon blue spots, they dart and dive and sparkle. What flyers they are. My encyclopedia says that dragonflies have sometimes also been called mosquito hawks, that *dragonfly* is the common name for an order of predaceous insects usually divided into two suborders, damselflies and true dragonflies. Do you remember all your childhood stories?—the boy and the giant, the frog and the princess, the dragon and the damsel. Those absolutes again.

A wren rattles among the cattails to my right. I think I've finally learned this year to separate the rattle of the marsh wren from the *ch-ch-ch-chirrr* of the sedge wren. There, the wren, it's noticed me, wants to get a better look, I make a squeaking sound with my lips against the back of my hand. Tail straight up, brown cap, strong white eye-stripe, black and white streaked back, it hops out onto the grass tips two metres away from me. A small but fierce bird, the marsh wren may puncture and eat the eggs of red-winged blackbirds or bitterns that disturb its territory. The male might build as many as six "dummy" nests in the marsh to encourage a female to choose him; but the female, after she has chosen, usually builds a nest of her own. Quick and active, secretive; I always feel lucky to see a marsh wren, any wren; lucky in love, despite the dour speculations of the *Winnipeg Sun*.

Rustling grass, loud grunt; a black-crowned night heron flies up suddenly nearby and startles me. It calls, and circles above. The bird world is full of surprises. Just two weeks ago, Susan and I chased up a black-crowned night heron on the Red River in Winnipeg; it was the 150th species we'd seen in two years in Riverview, a neighbourhood right near the centre of the city. Last year we saw one wood duck hen with forty ducklings on the river. We didn't know, she couldn't have hatched that many young on her own? Was she *babysitting* for other wood duck hens? We couldn't see other wood ducks around. This spring we found a mallard nesting in the crook of a tree eight metres above the swollen Red River. By the time the eggs hatched the river had fallen back within its banks, the young would have to tumble from the nest onto the hard ground. One morning near that same tree a year ago, I saw three different species of falcon—a kestrel, a merlin, a peregrine—in less than fifteen minutes.

Western grebe

I told a friend of mine last week over lunch that I found the writing life quite lonely, all that time I spend alone at my desk. She said I was lucky to be married, I would still have company evenings. She said that, single, sometimes she doesn't talk to anyone for four or five days; that worries her, she thinks the world may have left her behind. Beyond the hill and the bench where I snacked on my first visit, beyond the northeast curve, here on the southern boundary of the marsh, I have forgotten about loneliness. I think, now, maybe my lunch friend should come to the marsh with me at dawn. She would find that the marsh wren won't ignore her. That lesser yellowlegs might call, and she might answer. The wind might caress her while she wept. Two red-necked grebes slip below the surface of the water at the next bend. Somehow the marsh reminds you of all the things you've lost. Youth. Every day that's gone. My father's elevator. The train track. The well. Even memories fall away, there is only so much your thoughts can hold. Everything is lost. But everything is waiting too. That great blue heron waits, flies when it sees me coming. And that harrier, must have been resting at the water's edge, waiting for me at the pond edge.

Arkansas kingbird, Wilson's snipe, Audubon's warbler, myrtle warbler, long-billed marsh wren; my Icelandic friend, David, would have called that harrier a marsh hawk. "Old names are good names," he says, he keeps a kind of pride in remembering them, he doesn't like "armchair experts" changing bird names. Everywhere around me I hear rustling in the grass. Something waiting. Something still hidden. There's probably so much that I don't see, the marsh keeps its secrets well. Those four shorebirds that I've been tracking over the water, I call to them, I wish that they'd come back, stop nearby so I could name them. And they do. Here on the mud flat not six metres away. Sandpipers, peeps, much like the semipalmated earlier but with rufous markings on their backs and crowns. Western sandpipers—the first time I've seen this bird in Manitoba, they don't seem at all afraid of me—they've already flown five thousand kilometres from their nesting grounds. Most shorebird chicks hatch already covered in down and with their eyes open, only partly dependent on parents for food and care; they leave the nest within a few hours of hatching. Many run with their parents by the end of the first day and, as in the case of the western sandpiper, begin to take wing two or three weeks later; soon they will fly at eighty kilometres per hour to their wintering grounds.

What am I looking for here at the marsh? Wilderness? Something wild. Something wild in me. Looking for my other half, the one I lost a half-lifetime ago? Maybe, like the dragonfly nymph, I wait for some kind of transformation. I've tried to give myself up to this marsh, to surrender, to leave any plans behind. Tried the deadman's float so I could live again. Still, I tire. I know I have to find the car. I have to be back by a certain hour or Susan will wonder, send someone to find me. How can you give yourself to a marsh, a clutter of sedge grass and swamp? In the end, I've chosen where to walk, I've chosen what to see and what to name. I've chosen what to put on paper, what not. Nothing about copulation. Nothing about my own desire.

A sora calls, descending *coo-coo-coo-coo-coo-coo-coo-coo*. I remember the sora I watched at the north hill in spring several years ago, how it wandered in the puddles at my feet. The secretive sora. I filled with wonder that it would come so close, I could have touched it. Four great blue herons wave against the sky, I have never seen their nests in Manitoba. A merlin perches on a giant hay bale, flies up as I walk closer. I can smell the hay in this bale curing. A good smell. I think of all the hay I've handled, as a boy at home, as a teenager, as a young man, feeding cows or horses, I remember the *crunch* of cows eating. I watch nine pelicans in a domino line. They flap and glide, flap, flap, flap and glide. Murray tells a story of thirty pelicans he saw many years ago stretched in a shrinking half-circle in the water north at Grand Rapids, together they pushed the fish toward shore and finally ate them. A mosquito sings in my ear. Not one mosquito bite yet today, though I've heard or seen a half-dozen, my arms and legs still unprotected, almost four hours in the marsh. Superstition, even this close to the year 2000; I've been afraid to talk about mosquitoes, as though saying their name will draw them to me. I feel a bit foolish about that, and about the chemicals and netting I carry in my bag.

See the sow thistle. See the yellowlegs, the redheads on the water. See the whitetop in the sun, shining purple-brown. See the black tern, it seems to hunt over a field of barley, dipping, wheeling, diving. Is it really looking for insects, or just flying for the deep pleasure? *Keek, keek, keek, keek.* I'm sure these terns dislike people, they make such a fuss when we're around. They'll attack if you come near their nest, they can draw blood, I saw that up in Churchill. See how the coot pumps its neck as it swims. See the hawk circling far above me, Swainson's hawk, it drops lower, screams and screams, its mate answers, the two of them fly above me. Another late nest, I think. A warning, I should stay away from those trees a half kilometre to the south. I will listen; Swainson's hawks have been in trouble in Peru, dying by the hundreds from insecticides, I wish this family well.

I think my wandering in the marsh today has been less directional than two years ago. I stop. I look. I wander. I forget to check my watch. Still, in the last two kilometres I suddenly put a finger to my throat, touch the pulse on my throat. There; bump, bump, bump. I'm still here, still alive, still human enough to check my heartbeat. Ten beats in five seconds, ten times twelve, a good workout. And I'm still human enough to worry about the wasps that have gathered around me. What are they looking for, the granola bars in my knapsack, they shouldn't be able to smell that. We've got a wasps' nest growing under our wooden porch at home. I worried about that, visitors, the mail carrier. I thought I should probably destroy it. But then I read that wasps are good for gardens, they eat the insects that attack your plants. I've decided now, if those wasps don't bite us, we'll leave them alone.

Out in the marsh, out looking for birds, there's always a chance that you'll see something rare. A red-necked grebe always brings me pleasure. And a wren. The western sandpiper was unexpected, I can add that to my Manitoba list. It's hard to see new species these days in Manitoba, after the first 280; but I saw one other this year, with Susan, a western tanager on May 17 at a bird feeder near Kleefeld, brilliant red and yellow and black bird, must have been travelling to its summer home in British Columbia. Here comes a raven, flying toward me from the west, ravens, two of them. *Uuuurk.* Nothing unusual about the raven, though I like its rolling call. Jet-black raven, trickster raven. I doubt my father ever knew where he was going. I think he just walked a trail from clearing to clearing, pond to pond. I think he did well, he always managed to fit himself to the world around. Just like the merlin and the warbler, like my oldest sister long ago in Enterprise; here on the road, nearer the parking lot, one of those neon spotted dragonflies lies on its back in the gravel.

The end is always there around me. Inside me. Inside us. In that sense I suppose we all know where we're going. It's hard to know how to talk about writing. What it is. Fiction? Poetry? Essay? What it means. But listen. I'd love to tell you a story. This is the story of what happened to me. Like the milkweed, I too have a goal, to explode, to broadcast my words, my seed. Like the robin in spring, calling—*this is me, this is me*—I'm always singing my own song, no matter what else happens I keep singing my own song.

Prairie falcon

Weather Forecast

*P*eruvian fishing families have known about El Niño for at least a hundred years. They hatched the name, "boy child," for the warm ocean current that appeared off their coast each year before Christmas. They noticed in some years that this current turned exceptionally warm, that it stayed longer, and that it hurt their fishing. A hard life for families without fish—the irony of a name. Sir Gilbert Walker, studying the monsoon in India in the 1920s, suggested a relationship between the cyclical Indian droughts, occasional mild winters in Canada, and flooding in Peru; he faced ridicule for such an odd global approach to climate. It wasn't until the 1960s that scientists realized that those intense and persistent El Niños the fishermen talked about weren't just local Peruvian events, that they could be linked to weather patterns around the globe, that they brought increased rainfall in the southern United States and Peru, that they brought drought in India and Indonesia and huge brush fires in Australia, that Canadian winters turned suddenly warmer, that they were often followed by a corresponding cold La

Niña. They began to find evidence of El Niño reaching back more than a thousand years: in the corresponding growth rings of trees in Chile and Arizona, in the first written records of Spanish conquistadors in Peru, in the analysis of coral cores drilled in the Galapagos Islands. 1960s. Our current scientific models for studying and predicting weather patterns, especially as they relate to El Niño, are still remarkably underdeveloped.

All the talk this year is about the weather. On the TV, in community clubs, on the sidewalk, El Niño. Even at the cafe last night on Corydon Avenue where we gathered to celebrate one of Canada's most adventuresome poets, at Heaven Art and Book Cafe. We drank coffee and wine, we nibbled on pastries, we heard poems by bpNichol, and in the gaps between we talked about the weather. Talked about what beautiful weather we've been having this winter in Manitoba, temperatures hovering around zero Celsius now the last six or seven days, third week in February, must be some kind of new record we're setting. We talked about the sun; warm all winter, and that feels great, but the sun, we miss the sun. The warm temperatures have brought cloud cover, we Manitobans are used to far more sunshine. People turned from their tables and asked me about birds. "What's happened to the birds?" they said. Their bird feeders have hung deserted all through the winter, no flocks of siskins or redpolls, no house finches. What birds need feeders in this weather? El Niño.

Poems by bpNichol. I began to wonder last night about the shape of these essays, is there something I could do to make them come alive? Like El Niño, more intense, persistent, words that pound you, gut you, words that everyone would notice. How would Nichol have written about the marsh? I shouldn't even think about that, I find it hard enough to write in my own style and voice. But what if I just made lists, forgot about paragraph and syntax, about sentence structure? What if I just make lists; the things I see, my thoughts, my feelings, the words that jump onto my tongue, a long kind of poem:

dark
well, almost dark
wet road
stop sign
drive
black crow
wings
flap, flap, flap
blue car
rabbit
brake
tight
fear

The overriding feeling this morning as I drive to the marsh is one of fear. I'm afraid, just like the first trip. I don't know what I'll write when I get back to my computer. I don't know if I'll find anything to write, I feel that words will desert me. Writers talk about their fear of the blank page, I'm afraid of a blank marsh. Blank marsh? What would that mean? Nothing to see, nothing to do? My microcassette, a blank tape. It's not the tape that would go blank, stay blank, I know, or the page, or the marsh; I guess I'm worried about the writer.

In winter, if you step out at dawn, you see only two colours: snow and sky, a pale grey; barbed wire, fence posts, brush and trees and weeds, telephone poles, houses, they're black. That can last for an hour or more without sun, if it's cloudy. Rock doves this morning in the sky. And that old black crow. House sparrows in the shrubs when I walked from our back door to the garage, I heard them, they've started their courting dance, the males, their fanned tails. The wet streets remind me of April. Already I've noticed the daylight hours stretching. February. Still winter, even though it doesn't feel much like it. Winter. Winter wheat. Winterkill. Winterberry, of the holly family, probably not wild in Manitoba. Winter wren. What a delightful bird. I saw it first in British Columbia, hiking with Susan through forest in 1991; dark brown, noisy chatter, but still hard to spot in the underbrush. Saw one again here in Manitoba with a flock of warblers along the Red River in the fall a few years ago. Always low and in the shadows, I've never seen a winter wren in sunlight.

Winter. Frost. Frostbite. Snow. Snowbank, snowflake. Snowshoe hare, snow bunting. Himalayan snowcock, apparently they're established in the mountains of north-eastern Nevada, someday Susan and I will drive out to see them. Snow goose, snow leopard. Snowy egret and snowy owl. Snowmobile. I'd like to see a snowy owl today, sit down and watch it for a while. A few things I never knew about the snowshoe hare: that the young are born fully haired and with their eyes open, that they're able to run within a few minutes of birth, that's how hares are different from rabbits, rabbits are born naked and helpless. Great horned owl numbers fluctuate with the number of snowshoe hares, their favourite prey, a ten-year cycle. I never had much use for snowmobiles, loud, disruptive, they don't belong in the wild, or anywhere. I heard once that ranchers in Alberta liked to use them to run down coyotes, heard it straight from the rancher, but that was years ago. What did the four-teenth Dalai Lama say in the movie *Kundun* when the Chinese invaded with their guns and loudspeakers? "They have stolen our silence."

Just two or three kilometres south of Oak Hammock Marsh, I'm dreaming, driving on a gravel road and dream-ing, I wonder sometimes how drivers manage to stay on the road. I think about the marsh. What will I see today? Several years ago in late April I found Oak Hammock still cold and frozen when Winnipeg already looked like spring, snow gone and crocuses budding. Suddenly a snowy owl falls from a hydro pole in front of me—scares me, I lurch from my dream, brake hard—and snatches a mouse from the stubble, I get a glimpse of the mouse in its claws. The owl flies back up to the top of a hydro pole, a few seconds, the mouse is gone. Now, that owl sits there watching me, each of us watching the other. White throat, face, white undertail; top of the head, breast and belly white with dark bars. An immature, or a female, by the book. One, two minutes. The owl flies again, low above the ground and up to perch on a new pole two hundred metres away. I want to track it to see what it does. I inch my car closer, watch my odometer, till I'm about fifty metres away. The snowy watches me. Too close. It flies again, flashes white underwings, arches to the top of a pole behind me. From there it glares at me, yellow glare. Swivels its head to look away, turns to stare at me again. Then it seems to forget about me. I wonder if the owl can hear me as I ease down a window, as I shift in my seat, when I whisper onto my cassette. I watch. Wait. In the distance a raven calls. The wind soughs. Tips of dried grass quiver in the ditch. After a few minutes the owl flies again. Down across the road, across a field, it flies and flies, and up onto a fence post a half kilometre away, corner post of a small pasture. I watch through my binoculars. The owl sits. A magpie settles on the next fence post. The magpie waits, flies. The owl stays. Nothing else happens, though I watch for half an hour. I can see movement, the owl turning its head. I can't tell though whether it's still watching me, whether it's looking for mice. The magpie flutters nearby, from fence post to tree to hay bale, still in attendance, I hear it chatter.

Hawks. Owls. I watch them perched on their wooden posts, on electrical towers, hidden in trees, resting, waiting for prey. Such patient birds, they know how to wait, Barry Lopez in the desert. The way a writer sits in his chair and waits for words. Or maybe not. Daryl, when I tell him about my marsh project, raises his brows, his eyes brighten, a good idea. He asks what I do when I get there, do I find a good spot and wait? "No," I say. I guess that's what he'd do, he'd crouch and brew a pot of tea. "No," I say, "I'm not a *sitter*, I'm a *mover*." I'm not like a cat or an owl, I don't have the patience for stools or park benches. "No," I tell him, "most of the time I walk." Even my writing at home is more walking than sitting. As soon as my fingers stop on the keyboard I want to walk; I stalk around the house, into the living room, down the stairs and into the basement, hunting for nouns and verbs. Two ravens fly here over the road. I slow the car. Sometimes the easiest way to separate ravens from crows, if they're not calling, is to get the car directly below them, the shape of their tails so easy to distinguish then.

Misty this morning, the lines of sky and earth no longer so distinct. Cattle blend into pastures, magpies into brush, observer bleeds into observed. Not a dense fog, you can see for a mile in places, it builds and fades. The road feels soft under the car tires, rutting, especially the shoulders. The marsh, where I stop beside it, looks lifeless. Sprawls flat and open, clumps of naked trees blur on the horizon. I lock the car door. There. I do see open water though, something flying. Exciting. The snow has shrivelled and shrunk, settled. Melted. And frozen. Melted and frozen again, now a hard surface under my feet. I walk on the boardwalk into the willow bluff. Bushes and shrubs strip bare to their trunks, their branches, twigs. No birdsong. The only sound my feet on the hard snow, my boots *crunch* in the hard snow. A raven calls, *uurrrrck*, somewhere in the east. Calling for spring. The whitetop pale and golden. Dried weeds, and cattails, and wildflowers.

Stop . . . I think I hear a bird calling, a songbird. I listen, maybe the wind whistling in the trees.

I seem to use the word *weed* as a kind of throwaway; once I've named a plant that, I no longer need to pay attention. Maybe that's too easy, even stinking mayweed grows a brilliant flower. When I look in a dictionary under *weed* I find as a definition: *plants that grow where humans don't want them.* Certain encyclopedias have no entry at all for the word *weed*. Instead, they offer articles on *Weed Control*, articles largely about herbicides; they name white clover, both sweet-clovers, goldenrod, not as wildflowers but as weeds; they talk about greener lawns and better wheat crops. And on the Internet too. Yahoo suggests a large variety of Web sites on weed control, agricultural sites. But finally my search prevails, I find the right angle, native plants, the National Wildflower Research Center, news and information on North American native plants.

Somewhere a woodpecker hammers, downy or hairy by the time of year and habitat. Though I can't see it. *Tat-a-tat, tat-a-tat, tat-a-tat, tat, tat. Tat. Tat. Tat, tat-a-tat.* Working hard. I study the trees with my binoculars. I see dead limbs and old nest holes. With all that noisy work I should at least see wood chips and bark flying.

I thought the walking would be difficult here today, I thought the snow would be deeper, I thought I'd fall through. Maybe I'll get lucky, maybe this ice coating on the trail will persist. I leave the boardwalk and hike between heaps of brown mounded earth, Richardson's ground squirrel, a colony, still quiet here. I stop for a moment to check my cassette, make sure the batteries work. Yes, my voice, the crunch of my feet in the snow, I push the cassette player back in my pocket. A myriad of footprints here beside me. Human, boots. Rabbit, with droppings. Or probably hare, the white-tailed jackrabbit I now know, a member of the hare family. Some other creature too, small enough for a house cat, I wonder about fox. I imagine if it was muskrat I would see the belly or tail dragging. And possibly a weasel here, front and back footprints just two inches apart, much smaller than a house cat. The trail may be easy, still I find myself panting by the time I've walked half a kilometre.

Snow. Snow flurries. Snow squall. Heavy snow warning. The snow pops and scatters as I walk, in some places it's turned into sharp icy crystals. What do I know about snow? Peter Høeg's heroine, Miss Smilla, would have told me more about it; they say the Inuit have fifty different words for snow. So many ravens here. Groups of three or four. Or one alone. Calling and flapping. "Hey raven, *auurrck*," I call to one of them. "Follow me," I shout. One raven circles above, flies in front of me and around, swoops to the ground, calls back. I see a pale jackrabbit below it, the black tips of its ears, the jackrabbit bounces over a glare of ice and into the reeds and cattails on the other side. I bet I'll hear the sound of that raven again tomorrow at my desk. Here, sign of a raven walking, footprints etched hard in the snow.

Sometimes I've felt so cynical in my middle years, about the things that used to give us meaning—sunrise, love, religion, spirituality—contemptuous when people talk about them. It's the time we live in, I guess, God is always on *our* side. Maybe has something to do with Christmas too; greed and madness. The images we see on TV, many of them lies, lies all around us, everyone knows. And decisions, most often they seem based on economics rather than morality. Simple pleasure? Gone. Spontaneity? Some brand of mature innocence? The way a raven circles to get a second look at you when you shout. There is a contradiction to our bitter words, we're not cynical about the wild. Campers, cross-country skiers, hunters, snowmobilers all find some miracle of hope in the forest and sky and snow. Here's a bigger mammal now, a dog or a coyote. Two of the individual prints are smaller than the others, as though the front and hind feet differ in size. The bigger print with evenly spaced toes, four of them and a triangular pad; the smaller elongated, two toes in front, two on the outside, the pad wedging in the southeast corner. My animal footprint guide says that coyote, fox and dog prints are easy to confuse; that fox prints are, in fact, much bigger than a domestic cat's. You separate the three by watching their habits. The coyote travels straight and with a purpose; the fox follows elements of the landscape, a fence, the edge of a creek; a dog tends to wander.

Open water tracks across the ice on either side of me, marsh ice, white and gold and brown, a few darker spots the naked earth. The skies still overcast, monotone. I find goose droppings from the fall, oblongs where the snow has melted and shrunk or blown away. Drifts stretch in long snaking fingers across my trail. Grow deeper, and wide. My feet break through the icy crust, sink farther and farther down. I see the coyote has struggled with footing too, sinking to its belly in the snow. To the left of the dike, at the frozen water's edge, a flurry of feathers and bones in the snow, perhaps the last kill of the fall season, perhaps this same coyote. Here the walking is easier, the snow has caught on the dike, I can walk on the marsh, on the water. See how the ice cracks, how it rises and gullies, how it stains yellow and black and white. See this single dark feather, it's gathered enough heat inside to melt a circle in the snow. Now the dike rises above my head. I'm suddenly aware that no one will see me, that I'm hidden in the marsh, lost in the ice and the grass, the wind and snow.

Crunck, crunck, crunck, crunck. Hhhewhhaa, hhhewhhaa, hhhewhhaa. Sound of my breath on the tape, heavy breathing, I wish you could hear the sound of my feet and my breathing on this microcassette. *Crunckhhhewhhaa, crunckhhhewhhaa, crunckhhhewhhaa, crunckhhhewhhaa.* A breath line, a breath/step line. The poems of bpNichol.

I'd like to explain to you how these essays happen. I go to the marsh with my cassette, a small one, it fits in the palm of my hand, big hand. I wander and walk for four or five hours. I make notes on the cassette, the things I see and feel, the questions I ask, I'm just keeping lists after all. The next day I stay at home and transcribe, the transition from tape to essay takes almost a month sometimes, these essays probably the most difficult pieces I've written. I think of that process as working with raw material, shaping it, filling it. Still, you fill one glass and break another. If you could hear this tape now, two hours of tape, you'd be overwhelmed by the sound of my feet, by my hard breathing, words stuck between laboured breath, even the call of the ravens in comparison weak and far away.

I saunter farther along the ice edge. Someplace here the spot where I studied those western sandpipers as they fed and ran in the shallow water a half year ago, their beaks and rufous markings, the pleasure I felt at finding and identifying them. I notice that I'm in water too, six inches of water,

American coot

the ice won't hold me, I'll have to move back to higher ground. I stagger back up through accumulated snow and try the dike again, it seems more open now. I can see now how the snow moves around me. Where it gathers. Where it blows. Where it covers the dike. I can feel in my legs how the snow moves, my legs ache, they understand the snow's longing. Another footprint, elongated, rather pronounced claws, maybe a skunk that left its den to sniff and wander on a warm and winter day.

At the eastern boundary of the marsh, after a two-kilometre trek, I stop for a drink and a snack, apple and granola. I'm hungry. With all my clothes and my sack, my heavy boots, the snow, this hike far more difficult than in any other season. I pull off one of my shirts and sit for a while. Then I mark the coyote's scent with my own, a large rock. I turn into the north and the wind, and with that shirt rolled in my knapsack I feel again the chill of winter. Not much wind, standing still, but it strengthens as I push toward it. Five minutes' walking though cures the cold, hard to imagine after five minutes that it'll be another two months before the ducks and geese clamour on the water at Oak Hammock Marsh. I watch the whitetop here along the trail. Even without the wind these whitetop stalks lean far into the southeast. Prevailing wind. I watch for ravens but they've gone, left one magpie here calling. I watch for movement and mammals, find only a muskrat track, big foot, small foot, thin wavy tail. I walk and walk. I stumble on a rubber tire rut, water and a quarter inch of ice, I step through. I find horse droppings on a patch of dried trail. Horses, ruts, must have been wagon rides in fall.

The Cypress Hills country in southwestern Saskatchewan is notable for both its history and its geology. An area of hills, plateaus, gullies rising six hundred metres above the plain around it; one of the few regions of Canada not completely covered in the last large glaciation. The famous Mounted Police headquarters at Fort Walsh, Sitting Bull and the Indian troubles of the 1870s. Just two weeks ago I wandered those hills around Eastend with Seán. We followed a trail along a south slope across cattle range; grass and shrubs, dung and split prints and fluffs of hair hanging from bare brush. Seán pointed at raptor nests among the cliffs, he'd seen raptors there last spring. We walked, up and down, around outcroppings of rock, mule deer passed in front and behind, vanishing here, showing there again. Our trail bent north, skirted a deep coulee, a stand of tall conifers, white spruce, lodgepole pine. I thought: birds. We called, both of us. *Shpishh, shpishh.* Chickadees, red-breasted nuthatches, common redpolls flew and gathered and clamoured around us; a magpie, of course; even a woodpecker somewhere on the periphery. Toward dusk we sat for a while among the aspen higher on the slope, a fallen trunk. And as we turned for home a coyote stood suddenly on a ridge above us. Yip and howl, coyotes singing all around us. I stopped. I wanted to watch that coyote, I couldn't take my eyes off that coyote, the way he figured the sky. I felt a gnawing pain. "Sure," Seán said, he might have heard me thinking, "he's watching, he's wondering about us." A part of me wanted to run with that coyote. Hey, coyote! I wanted to shout. Look at me! I love you, coyote. I wanted to be that coyote, wild like him. I thought for a moment, maybe if I died and came back I would like to be a coyote.

Some scientist on CBC Radio not long ago talked about the next ice age. He said that the last ice age had begun to recede only fifteen thousand years ago, not that long, and that the next ice age would come. "We don't know when," he said, "but we know it will come." Presaging the death of this planet, of the sun, of the species, all the species. Maybe that's part of our pain, our gnawing pain, the fear of death coming, looking that far into the future. The flame of a welder's torch, heating a joint on a hay feeder or a calving pen. My father told me, growing up, that welding flame was dangerous. "Don't look at it," he said, "it'll burn your eyes."

Mammals, all those tracks I've seen. I stop and turn my ears. I hear sounds around me. An airplane, small one. A car, or a truck, in the distance. A magpie. I hear my microcassette winding. There, something screaming. Sounds almost like the call of a hawk or eagle. I scan the northeast horizon with my binoculars. Some creature, low, and in the grasses, I think. Sounds injured. If I could find movement somewhere I might go take a look. Ahh! Fox! Black legs and ears. Red in the neck, chest, shoulders. More grey behind, even in the tail, and a white tip. Running along the eastern dike. And another. Must be their call. Are they mating? What have these foxes been doing this winter? Do they burrow and sleep? Maybe not this winter, food easy to find. I watch the two foxes run for a hundred, two hundred metres along the dike, till they disappear, still calling, on the other side.

Snow. It gathers. And pocks, and stretches. It piles, waxes and wanes. It tracks and trails. It falls and blows and drifts. It did. It melts again. Two hours into the trail another raven; this one I can't call back, though I try, it's set on its own adventures. Now the breeze has gone I feel quite warm, I think of a shortcut across the ice. Is that foolish? Would the ice hold? How deep is the water? I find some green left here in the clearing at my feet, quack grass, small shoots of clover, from last year. Out in the marsh today not much to distract me from my dazed walking. Dream walking. Maybe the prairie winter does that, puts you to sleep. Ten minutes after eleven, I left the car at nine, I think I've come about halfway. The snow goose has very little to do with snow. Except that it's white, that it nests in the Arctic, in the land of snow. It appears as the snow leaves, departs when the snow comes again, in its habits the antithesis of snow. Snow buntings winter in Manitoba. They're white too. You see them in flocks of a hundred drifting over last year's wheat fields, feeding along the road. They burrow in snow to keep warm. The hoary redpoll might have been called a snowy redpoll, colour and range. The snowy egret, so far south, how did it get its name?

I haven't tried my shortcut yet. Haven't found one that looked right. I finished my trail-mix at ten, and my apple, I still have a few carrots and a bottle of water. Now I see the western boundary of my trail ahead, a welcome sight. There should be muskrats nearby. From where I stand, eleven, twelve muskrat lodges. Muskrats apparently spend a lot of time in their lodges, huddled together, the thick layer of plant stems and snow keeping them warm; they enter the water even in winter to find food, breathe at push-ups they build in the ice. Their first litter of the season will be born in April or May. My shortcut across the ice, there it is past this muskrat lodge, at the northwest corner of my trail. I'll try it. The ice seems good, strong enough. But the snow beyond it, among the brush and thistle and clover, is far deeper than I expected.

I'm wet from my journey. And I'm tired. I still feel the chill of late winter. The plants and grasses rustle under my feet. Except for that, silence. Even the wind has died. I walk, and walk. South, and still south. Walking becomes automatic, I don't even think anymore. I note, in my stupor, the stream from the artesian well open and rippling here beside me. But I'm too tired to stop, think only of the car and the parking lot. Suddenly, a squawk, and three mallards fly up beside me. Then a dozen more, two dozen, mallards that have stayed this mild winter. Snowy owls, in years when lemmings are abundant in the Arctic, may incubate as many as fifteen eggs, other years they may not nest at all. In winter they sometimes follow and feed from flocks of ducks.

Just after Eastend I visited a school in Saskatchewan with a large black-and-white photograph of Martin Luther King, Jr. hung on a classroom wall, his friends and supporters crowding around him. The students knew what he was about, I questioned them, they knew his marches and his boycotts and his people. As a youth, I heard King speak on the radio, on TV. *I have a dream that one day on the red hills of Georgia . . .* Potent words for the '60s—those years of love and freedom, of vision and rebellion—everyone heard them, felt their power, for, or against. King's voice, his words still thrill me, shiver my spine, I have them here on my computer, one twitch of the index finger away, maybe the last great voice we heard. Of course, my parents were not descended from southern slaves. Nor were they Native American; wrong time, wrong place, wrong blood. But I think of the Native traditions of sweat lodge and vision quest; their birthright of fasting and solitude, sacred song and ground, the dreams that gave them meaning. I think of those dreams and songs and visions; I wish sometimes those ancient spirits would call to me.

Great blue heron

Pelican's Pouch

I remember as a boy reading about the desert, the Sahara Desert, probably geography texts and children's novels, school encyclopedias, I liked all of those; maybe my interest was fuelled by Sunday school stories about Moses and the Israelites, all those years they spent wandering in the wilderness. Deserts held such unique qualities for boys, girls too I'm sure. Sand dunes, sandstorms, nomads, camels, oases, goatherds and herders; even then I was a stock farmer at heart. Flowering plants that lived start to finish for just two or three days, right after the rain, seeds having lain dormant for years; animals that knew how to control the rate of their own heartbeat and metabolism, had to know to survive, the horned toad. What would you wear? Sometimes, in the desert, the temperatures swung from fifty-two degrees Celsius in the daytime, in the shade, to below freezing at night. I imagined pure sand, beach sand, stretching for hundreds and thousands of miles; and I remember rocks and mountains too, places for robbers to hide. I didn't read that seriously, I commissioned the words as catalysts for my mental travels. Desert, the perfect wilderness for any young dreamer.

Certainly, Florida is no desert, and wilderness there may be difficult to find, still I gained some appreciation for sand and its movement while walking the beaches on its east coast. Singer Island. Morning. My first day in Florida, ever, we didn't even stop for breakfast, our hosts still snored in their bed. I wanted to get out, see what this new landscape might propose, I rushed Susan along. Of course, we took our binoculars. Laughing gulls, ring-billed gulls, a few herring and Bonaparte's gulls. Brown pelicans diving from the pier. Royal and sandwich terns, and Forster's, maybe one roseate tern. And black skimmers. Killdeers. Sanderlings running at the waves' edge. Eurasian collared-doves and mourning doves in among the buildings, and a peregrine hunting from the crown of a twenty-five-storey condominium. I wore a pair of tan shorts, even though the air was still cool, the sky low and moving fast, I wanted that Hollywood-brown skin too. We walked for an hour or two along the beach, Susan and I, she fell behind a few times, picked up some old shells. I wondered at first why the calves of my legs hurt. Couldn't be sunburned yet. No, it was the wind, southeast wind, blowing off the ocean in the morning and whipping the sand against the backs of my legs. Sandstorm. Sand sting. I watched how the sand had begun to drift overnight behind the cabanas, foot-high and five-foot-long sand dunes on the lee side of their arched blue canopies. I thought, like snowdrifts, Manitoba, nothing new. The first days that beach sprawled wide and almost level, but the wind and waves, by the end of the week, had cut the banks and pushed the sand into sharp dunes and ridges. Wedge, and crest, and shoal; that beach, my brother-in-law told me, from one day to the next didn't ever really look the same.

You might see the red-cockaded woodpecker fly in the pinewoods a hundred times, undulating flight, from a hundred different angles, and never see the red feather tuft behind its eye. You might hold the kinglet in the belly of your hand and never see its ruby crown. You might watch three painted bunting females at the feeder, you might wait till dusk and never see the gaudy male. That's the beauty of this experiment, always some small mystery left still undiscovered. If you visit Florida for the first time and you drive your rental Malibu across the peninsula, through the fragrant and blossoming orange groves, to the Gulf Coast and into Fort Myers, you'll see more long-legged wading birds than you ever thought possible. Cattle egrets parade on driveways and porches and front lawns. Snowy egrets stroll in the ditches. Great egrets rest on the boulevards, breeding season, their delicate trailing plumes. Great blue herons thread the long sky. Little blue herons feeding on the beach; and reddish egrets dancing, wings arched, their wild and lunatic dance. Roseate spoonbills scan the sloughs and marshes. Flocks of glossy and white ibises gather round ponds, brilliant colour, and their down-curved bills. Wood storks wade and grope with their broad beaks in the coastal shallows.

We stopped and watched some of those herons while they hunted. The green heron in the marsh at the Loxahatchee National Wildlife Refuge, hunting just two metres from where we stood exposed on an earth dike. It stalked, and waited among the marsh grass. Stepped. Extended its neck. Waited again. It picked a fish out of the water, tossed it in the air for a better grip. Swallowed it, two-inch minnow. It ran three metres along the dike and began to stalk again. The great blue heron thirty metres farther along the trail tried much bigger prey. The fish it chose, longer than its beak, didn't want to go down, it got stuck in the heron's throat, struggled there while the heron twisted and stretched its pencil neck. And we watched a brown pelican fishing too, alongside the anglers and rods and reels on Sanibel Island. Instead of flying above the waves and diving, it floated on the water and caught the fish thrown back by the fishermen, one of those fish so big and strong, the way it struggled Susan thought it would surely tear that pelican's black pouch. Plunge divers, those brown pelicans. We've heard that brown pelicans eventually go blind from the impact, the way they fall from as high as twenty metres, crash against the water.

Tigertail Beach near Naples, Florida, on a Wednesday morning. Wilson's plovers, semipalmated plovers, black-bellied plovers, snowy and piping plovers and killdeers; ruddy turnstones and dunlins, sanderlings and willets, least sandpipers, western sandpipers, semipalmated sandpipers, short-billed dowitchers, lesser and greater yellowlegs; hundreds and thousands of shorebirds feeding on an expanse of sand. Corkscrew Swamp Sanctuary in the afternoon; six thousand acres, four kilometres of boardwalk. Through pine flatwoods, wet prairie, cypress forest. The plants. Slash pine. Cabbage palm. Bald cypress. Saw palmetto. Yellow-eyed grass. Golden polypody. Star-topped sedge. Buttonbush. Strangler fern. Alligator flag. Old man's beard lichen. Broad-leaved arrowhead. The sanctuary field guide we bought at the entrance proved invaluable in telling us about the varieties of vegetation. And along the eastern beaches, tropical hardwood hammocks, the old Florida. Red mangrove. Bahama nightshade. Nickerbean. Jamaica caper. Spanish stopper. Sea-grape. Gumbo limbo. Pigeon plum. Nickerbean, I can't imagine where that name would come from. Or polypody. I like to roll those words over my tongue again and again, Spanish stopper, pigeon plum. All of them, what captivating names. Now that I'm home, with spring coming, I need to find out more about the plant life here, in my own province. What are the exciting plant names of the prairies?

In southwest Florida, double-crested cormorants perch in rows on power lines along the road like Winnipeg starlings; red-shouldered hawks hunt and soar like Manitoba red-tails, swallow-tailed kites traverse the sky like giant barn swallows. Sometimes, driving the gravel roads through the Everglades, we were surprised by the landscape, fields opening wide on one side of the road, suddenly no palms, no saw palmetto. But a meadowlark singing from a scrub, American goldfinch in a quiver of willows, a loggerhead shrike in a naked tree, a herd of cattle. We felt as though we were driving in southern Manitoba, that Florida landscape almost like the patches of wood and pasture and cattle Susan and I passed minutes before the storm and our burrowing owls near Melita just two years ago.

The more places you see, the more one reminds you of the other. I'm in the car now and on my way to Windygates.

Windygates? It's actually marked on my Manitoba map, and I've been near there a dozen times, though I've never yet seen the town. Good two-hour country drive south and west from Winnipeg. It's the name used by local birders for a spot in southern Manitoba they like to visit when spring threatens, early April. You drive down into the Pembina River valley and you watch hawks and eagles sailing north in droves. Another spring migration. Hawks and eagles, falcons, herons, cranes, ducks and gulls, robins. Windygates.

Seven a.m. I drive south along Pembina Highway. If I look between buildings and through gaps in trees toward the east and the Red River, I see that the sun has just begun to show. The sky almost covered in thin cloud, I expect it will clear in an hour or two. Both rivers are swollen today— the Red, where it bends to border the road in St. Norbert; and the La Salle, where the bridge crosses—though nothing like last year, there'll be little flooding, the Red River crested this year almost a month earlier than last. Last year we didn't talk much about swollen rivers, we talked about lakes. Still south, on Highway 75; sun, on the left, glaring in my eyes, everywhere the signs of spring coming. Snow melted. Water in the ditches. Fields open and drained, waiting for the seed drill, the tractor. Crows in pairs, and gulls flying over. Geese. I can't see any green showing though; nor any buds, bushes and trees still suspicious of this year's early warm weather. Still distrustful of El Niño.

I pass a dark-phase hawk perched on a hydroelectric

pole. The Red River just like Windygates; this is the time of year when hawks fly in large numbers along river valleys from the south into Manitoba. Something to do with how the air moves, thermals; the way currents of warm air, no matter how slight, rise from river valleys and along ridges, provide a cushion for the hawks to glide on. The early sun shines on the face of a west ridge, catches the dark husk of trees, heat gathers, a draft develops. Of course, the trees and the river also mean prey, and a good place to roost. Some years hawk watchers in southern Manitoba have counted as many as eight hundred hawks travelling up one river valley in a day. This year seems to be a bit different though, no big accumulations of hawks. With all the snow melted on the land and the river ice already thawed, maybe the air currents have changed. And the hawks too, maybe they've spread their flight paths, in time and space. Here, north of Ste. Agathe, a red-winged blackbird settles on a signpost.

A year ago this highway lay deep under water, water stretching for miles on either side, and down into the United States, Grand Forks. I still see the signs of that flood, that great flood. Piles of sandbags behind buildings, in low-lying areas of farmyards. Heaps of stained drywall, old studs, insulation, even kitchen cupboards, waiting to be carted away. Garbage and pieces of shed where the floodwaters deserted them in shelter belts. Houses still being built, or repaired, or raised to put them far above any possible future flood level. We hope. Bulldozers, and permanent earth dikes still being pushed into place and packed. Families and lives in disorder. There's a house mounded at least six metres above the field around it. And here, here's the bridge to Aubigny, where a tornado landed a few years ago, tore some old trees and granaries apart.

Today's a Wednesday. I feel pretty lucky to be out here while my friends slave in their offices or factories, their schools, some looking for jobs. Of course, I'm working too. I'm writing. Researching. Sort of. I feel pretty lucky to be out here at all, having escaped all the natural and other disasters

130

American white pelicans

that have touched down around me: fire, and famine, and flood, disease. Lucky to see another spring. Lucky. Like that horned lark there on the shoulder of the highway, the way it bobs and twitters as it flies, the sound of tinkling glass. I'm surprised this morning how few horned larks I've seen, with this weather they should be everywhere along the road. There's a pair of mallards though, just off the highway. And a cat in the ditch, hunting, domestic, a half mile from the nearest yard. A meadowlark singing on an electric wire. Not that I can hear that meadowlark from inside the car as I drive by, but I see his profile against the sky, round and stubby body, the way he always lifts his head to sing.

There's a red-tailed hawk. And another hawk, hunting. A third, I stop the car to have a look. Rough-legged hawk. Spattered, and mottled, with black feathers and pale, dark belly-band, belted white tail. On the pole where it probably spent the night. Hawks apparently don't migrate at night, though many smaller birds do, warblers and kinglets and sparrows; they migrate at night when the hawks can't find them. The prairie unfolds all around me. East edge of the Pembina Triangle, where so many Mennonite immigrants from Ukraine settled in the 1870s, where my Mennonite ancestors followed after the Bolshevik Revolution, soon after the collectivization of Stalin. Winkler, Altona, Carman, some of the richest farmland in Western Canada. Grain. Another rough-legged hawk. As I pull back onto the highway a truck with a semitrailer full of Charolais cattle roars by.

Morris, Manitoba, squeezed between the banks of the Red River and the Morris River, half hidden behind its flood dike. Morris, first called Scratching River, maybe because of the mosquitoes, maybe the poison ivy on the river shore. The Morris River swollen too. In the middle of town I turn west on Highway 23. By now the sun has risen, and fallen again it seems, disappeared behind a curtain of cloud; the sky completely overcast, despite our forecast for sun. Here, along the 23, mallards dabble in the ditches. They fly above in pairs. They swerve. They call and court and mate. Springtime in Manitoba; if you see a puddle of water and cattails, marsh grass, you should expect to see mallards and red-winged blackbirds. A Manitoba joke. Some of the earliest spring migrants to return to their summer homes, red-winged blackbirds travel in huge flocks mixed with brown-headed cowbirds, Brewer's blackbirds or grackles; you see swarms of them swirling against the sky, especially in fall. Lots of red-winged blackbirds here, males, singing, territories memorized and waiting for their mates, those mates always a few days behind. I notice bits of green growing around them in the ditches and fields, and there, a pale northern harrier flying. Now, ahead of me, I catch a shadow ridge of hills against the west horizon, the Pembina Hills. West and north of the Red River the land rises in an escarpment—the plateaus of the Pembina, Turtle, Riding, and Duck Mountains—once shaping the western banks of the ancient Lake Agassiz, the Pleistocene epoch.

Road signs. Junction Highway 3. I need to turn left again. At the red stop I roll down my window, breathe some fresh air, listen to the killdeers calling around me. Five or six years ago, in the first week of April, Susan and I watched how the snow geese gathered by the thousands in the fields east of Morden. That was early in our birding life, we had never seen so many geese in one place before, and the way they shone when they flew up against the sun, we watched and wondered. Those geese fly up around me now, off the corn stubble, hordes of them, snow geese again, blue and white phases. Highway 3. I cross Shannon Creek. Cross Dead Horse Creek. Suddenly the fields are wet again, still hold pools of water. When I turn to Morden, it feels as though the road slowly drops in front of me. Probably not true, probably just the magic of the hills rising up ahead. I watch for trunk and provincial road signs, something to orient me on my way back from Windygates. Manitoba Provincial Road 432; a possibility, runs north and south. That red-tailed hawk flying just above it with a mob of crows chasing behind. Manitoba Provincial Road 434. I always end up coming home cross-country, I wonder if one of these would bring me back.

Driving west out of Morden the highway begins to climb, the prairie develops a soothing roll. Hills. Coulees. Brush gathers and thins. Small stands of aspen and bur oak assemble in bluffs and in creases. A sign, *Pembina Valley Conservation District*. More snow on the ground here, and lots more water, alongside the road, in the fields. And mud, the fields look like mud. Still, some of the brush-lines and windbreaks show a distinct orange or brown-red hue, maybe the buds starting to open. A hawk flies north over the road, short and rounded wings, accipiter; Cooper's hawk, I would bet by the curved tail in the sky above me. Another sign, *Pembina Crossing*. My dictionary tells me that the word *pembina* refers to a variety of cranberry, a highbush cranberry, presumably wild. Is that what these hills and valleys were named for, a berry? Saskatoons, gooseberries, cranberries, buffalo berries, all a strong part of the prairie culture, blueberry picking. My cutoff here? Yes. Junction 31. The town of St. Claude, that's the big rock there in the southeast quarter. This is where I leave Highway 3, turn south toward Langdon, a small town on the other side of the U.S.-Canada border.

The first time I made this trip I had difficulty finding my way, the time with Susan and the snow geese, someone had told us to use the "big rock" as a landmark. "Turn south at the big rock," he said, he didn't remember the numbers on the highway. But it seemed, west of Morden, that all the south turns had rocks piled around them, we had to try each one. This road, 31, bends and curls; that's something for Manitoba, its reputation for straight roads. A paved road, though it's getting pretty rough, pocked and pitted; the economy of the 1980s and '90s has been hard on Manitoba highways. This country south of Highway 3, in its contour, sets out to imitate the hills of Eastend, Saskatchewan, though imitate only. This is still farmland more than range, tilled and sown and harvested rather than fenced. Here a ring-billed gull flies north. And another. Now, suddenly a sign ahead, a steep hill. I bump through another rough spot in the road and begin my descent.

Down. And down. And down.

Oh! There! A flock of wild turkeys, maybe twenty of them, in a clearing just thirty metres off the road. Cocks with their blue heads and blood-red wattles, dark beards hanging from their breasts. Plumage in gold and green and bronze, barring in black and white; five male turkeys with their tails fanned. *Gabblgabblgabblgabblgabbl!* What grandeur. The hens, nonchalant, pick at the ground for seed, oblivious to the males' posturing. Permanent residents of these hills; after the winter, when the sexes wander in separate flocks, the males' gobbling brings the females in to mate. Such giant birds, so magnificent to watch, they wander off into the woodlands west of the clearing when I stop, I hear them calling long after they've disappeared.

The slopes around me cover in trees, oak and aspen

again, and Manitoba maple; rocks bulge among them. To the south I see the valley stretching east and west, the river turning. I meet another flock of turkeys, three cocks here, nine hens. Dark-eyed juncos gather along the road in front of the car. They swarm on the gravel and pick for seeds, they fly as I roll closer, the flash of their white tail feathers. When I stop, they gather again. Four, maybe five dozen juncos, and a sprinkling of chipping sparrows; even the movement of my arm is enough to scatter them. A fox sparrow settles and calls from a bush. The wind soughs. Farther down the valley the land has gone wild. Fences here, pasture, though some of the lines have fallen. I park the car just beyond the bridge. I pull out my binoculars, survey the posts and wires for bluebirds, any trip to Windygates incomplete without a mountain bluebird.

Pembina River, swollen too. The Pembina flows south from here, and then east to join the Red just below the border. The water gushes and curls and eddies, spins around rocks, lunges along cutbanks. Logs and branches, drifted dead trees bunch on the shale bars. A killdeer calls in the east. A kingfisher rattles, and dives. A wood duck weaves and disappears behind some brush. A song sparrow drops from a willow onto the ground along the riverbank, its dark stripes and markings, just the kind of habitat where you often find them nesting. Bald eagles flap and glide, circle far above me. Three, four. Six of them, only one mature, white head and tail, the others with pale blotches on their underwings. The eagles join and spin around each other. Two killdeers to the northwest. More snow geese overhead, hundreds. A pair of mallards again. I wander through a pasture, a cattle trail, still along the river, and into a stand of willows, dried willow leaves hanging from the branches. Hoof prints on the trail, deer, and droppings, on a sandy soil, washed into place by centuries of spring flooding.

No bluebirds anywhere. I get back into the car and drive up onto a plateau. Up again, and out of the valley. More farmland; grain, from the stubble. And three tundra swans, black legs, black beaks, long necks stretched, slow lumbering flight when you see them this close to the ground. And ten more swans, they must have settled for the night in a field beyond that ridge. I pass the 201 cutoff east to Osterwick where I usually turn for the hawk count, and continue south. I check my map, must be just a few kilometres to the border from here, just a few kilometres to Windygates. Less than that. There's the Customs area, the border, but still no mention of a town. The prairie, one red-tailed hawk, a brown-and-white building, a black truck. The Customs officer tells me that this is Windygates. "There isn't much else to know, used to be a settlement here many years ago." I'd like to ask her more questions but she's holding a portable phone, impatient to get rid of me.

I turn the car around. *Welcome to Bienvenue au Manitoba.* One hundred and eighty-four kilometres from Winnipeg. The 201 is a gravel road, almost; more like mud today, soft. It dips and levels, dips and rises, runs between stubble and slough. Mud spatters on the underside of the car, past my side driver's window, front-wheel drive. The road falls again, deeper this time, the car begins to slide. I feel nervous about this drive, I'm glad Susan isn't here, just one set of nerves to deal with. I pass horned larks singing. And more tundra swans, flying. Pass a wood-frame building, brick chimney, moss growing on the grey and wooden shingles, two-by-fours angled on the east side, no bigger than my single-car garage at home. *Chicken Hill School Division #581, 1892-1962,* a schoolhouse braced against time. By now bright sun, the clouds have faded. The 201 leaves the farmland, bends back into trees and brush. A woodpecker hammers. A blue jay calls. Fox sparrow again, its pleading tones. And a chickadee. Last spring in Winnipeg the fox sparrows sang along the river while we threw sandbags in the backyards of homes on Kingston Crescent, we were lucky, all those houses were saved. On that pond below the poplars, a pair of mallards, a pair of wood ducks, and one female hooded merganser, thin bill and feathers stretching at the back of her head.

The road, as I drive back down into the valley, gets even worse, wet and rutted, I have to work to stay away from the shoulders. A steep road. Scary in these conditions, though from the ruts there's been some traffic. I drive down and down. Mud. And dry patches. Mud again. By now the windows on the right side of my car covered in mud so I can barely see. Suddenly a dozen turkeys on the road in front of me. They scatter as I slide by. Down, and finally to the Pembina River again, the car idles across the bridge. The traction going back up is much the same, first gear, rocks waiting to greet me on either shoulder, if this road got any worse I'd have to spend the night. A dry spot ahead of me. I stop the car, pull up the brake, turn the front wheels so if the car rolls it'll butt against the bank behind, and turn off the ignition. Eleven-thirty. I step from the car, set up my scope and my tripod, and wait.

Hawks circle high above me. One red-tailed. Two sharp-shinned, so small beside the red-tail. And a Cooper's. A third sharp-shinned hawk settles in a bur oak beside me. A northern harrier curls by, circles and stalls. The northern harrier is a common bird across the prairies, around swamps and sloughs, pastures. A slim bird, the male usually pale grey, the female brown, both have a conspicuous white rump patch and a long tail. They fly low over the ground while hunting, twist and spin, have been observed hovering in front of a prairie fire waiting to pick off any mice that try to escape. While many hawk pairs seem to stay together for life, some harrier males take more than one mate in a season.

Here on the east ridge of the Pembina River valley hundreds of robins have gathered. They whistle and call, fly from tree to tree, north, always north, soon they're gone. One male hairy woodpecker follows them. Just south of the car a rock face—thirty, sixty metres—veins of stratified rock, gnarled roots of trees, and bits of shale clattering down to the road; six ring-billed gulls appear over the trees at the top of that rise. A second red-tailed hawk falls from the west ridge and into the valley. And another, sailing straight north, it comes, it's gone, so fast. A fourth red-tail. And a crow, circle and weave. A dozen passerines fly above, robins maybe. And four more raptors on the west ridge, too far away to name even with a telescope. One rough-legged hawk. The wind gathers and sighs; sometimes when a calm settles around me, sweater and jacket, the sun feels almost warm. Waiting for hawks. Time slows and drags. Waiting, such a difficult game. I think of the Inuit hunters, how long they waited beside their holes in the ice, harpoon in hand, waited for seals to appear, hours without moving. Their lives dependent on their patience.

A red squirrel chatters behind me. I turn for a better view. It rustles along branches, through weeds and leaves, disappears into a ravine. Listen! The *chuck* of a hermit thrush. I climb down into a hollow after the squirrel and sit for a while beside a brook. Water gurgles and bubbles and falls, so noisy down here I probably wouldn't notice if a car passed on the road, if somebody picked up my scope and ran.

Twelve-thirty. One hour, long enough to sit in one place, I have other things to do, places to see. I lay the tripod and scope on the back seat of the car, the car labours to start up the hill again. It slips and roars, grabs. I rise from the valley to find white-tailed deer grazing in the stubble. More mud and water on the road. I pass a pair of greater scaups on a pond; his round head, greenish sheen, grey-blue bill, her bold white facial patch. I pass kestrel and sparrow, another red-tailed hawk, a male hooded merganser. Farmland. Rises and gullies. The road bends.

Sometimes in spring the movement of geese isn't that easy to understand. You see great flocks flying south or east instead of north, they don't always fly in the direction they're supposed to. Maybe they lose their way, maybe they're just smarter than we think. I wish now I had a snow goose sitting here beside me, maybe it could tell me how to get home. I wish I had a pelican's pouch full of maps. I haven't seen any road signs since the valley. 432. 434. Nothing. I don't know where I'm going. The road just seems to get muddier. I come up against dead ends. I check my one map. I'm not even sure of my directions anymore. Which is north? I'm navigating by the seat of my pants, I hope these pants don't betray me.

When I step from my house in Riverview one morning later that week, two dozen juncos fly from under our feeders, they must have found their way from the Pembina River. I hear the whistle of mourning dove wings, catch a flash of the fox sparrow hiding in the box elder. A starling flies in the neighbour's yard. Black-capped chickadee calls. Mallards chase above the treetops. Robins sing, ruby-crowned kinglets warble; the pleasure of living just four houses from the Red River, you do see more birds along the river. A friend of mine tells me, in his yard, the first house finch and chickadee nests fledged a few weeks ago; birds taking advantage of the weather, the earlier they nest the stronger the young will be for winter, the sooner the first young fledge the easier for the parents to raise another brood.

I walk west along Ashland Avenue, homes almost fifty years old, away from the river, under the American elms, elm buds shining and golden in the rising sun, swollen, waiting to burst into leaf. More birds overhead, three northern flickers—the glimmer of yellow in their wings—common grackles, pine siskins, one ring-billed gull, a red-winged blackbird, yellow bellied sapsucker flying from elm to spruce. I hear a falcon somewhere hunting; a merlin pair nests every year in Riverview, it's probably one of them. I cross Darling. Cross Eccles. Mabel, Fisher, Casey. I wander along back alleys, stop to look in yards, after a few years you get to know where the feeders are, where the birds congregate; birds still gather below feeders even in spring, sparrows and juncos, crack the leftover seeds of winter. I pass an old purple martin house where house sparrows couple on the runways; one house sparrow male mounts his mate again and again, must be ten or twelve times in a minute, his instinct tells him to make sure.

Clusters of aging oak in the older blocks of Riverview, scraggly and wild compared to the elms, twisted, and more spruce and cedar, the homes almost a hundred years here. I notice a thrush flying, hermit, or Swainson's, grey-cheeked. Secretive birds, hard to locate by their call, thrushes often skulk in the undergrowth, they seem to take wing as soon as you get a clear view of their eye. Reddish-brown tail on this one, hermit thrush. Suddenly, tundra swans trumpeting in a long line overhead. Twenty-three tundra swans. The first time I've ever seen them over Winnipeg. The corner of Casey and Ashland, at the red-breasted nuthatch house, the yard where I'm most likely to see a red-breasted nuthatch in winter.

Just short of Osborne Street I turn south onto a back alley. Here, the noise of the traffic grows louder, buses and cars, eight o'clock, people on their way to work. Still, I hear a chickadee whistling, same call as the first two notes of the white-throated sparrow song. When I started learning bird songs I thought I heard the white-throated sparrow singing at my house every morning one February. So early in the season, I told Susan. Then I was embarrassed when it proved to be a black-capped chickadee; I discovered my mistake while listening to a tape of recorded bird songs, mistakes can be a very good way to learn. Closer to the Red River I see crows in fours, a flock of rock doves where they roost under the Osborne Bridge, I hear killdeers calling. Oak trees here, and ash, cottonwood, box elder, dogwood, elm, last year's leaves still thick under my feet. I wander along the river trails. A white-breasted nuthatch calls. A pair of wood ducks, in a puddle where the snow gathered in a hollow and then thawed, they're worried about me. Look at his brilliant colour, his red eye, red on his bill, the way white borders the green on his crest and his wings. And a hawk. I've scared up a hawk. Cooper's, female, in that cottonwood. A pair. The male crouched on a pile of branches and twigs near the top of a dead ash. Farther along, blue jays, it's astonishing how quiet blue jays can be when they're on a nest.

I walk east through the trees and brush along the river-bank. I hear a woodpecker hammering. Sometimes you just can't find those woodpeckers, even when they're hammering and in full view. I see him now though, a male downy, I watch how he rattles and shakes on his branch. And there's his mate. What a fuss they make, calling, and flying at each other, one chasing the other up a tree trunk. Something dark and furry splashes at my feet, leaves circles in the brown water, beaver, or muskrat, I imagine. Some years beavers stop here along the river and cut down trees, dozens of trunks cut, a lot of damage to the trees. City workers drive out in their trucks and wrap the trees in chicken wire, I've heard they trap the beavers and haul them away. My trail here covers in wet silt, the receding water levels, my shoes are getting heavy. I see dog prints beside mine. And others as well, triangular with long claws. I fish for the wildlife footprint guide in a pocket and find instead my wristwatch. Almost nine-thirty, I have an appointment, I need to get home; my time has flown while I wandered here along the river.

That's how spring comes again to Manitoba. The passage of time. Two dozen swans in the sky; an American coot at the water's edge; brown creeper searching a tree trunk, climbs up, flies down, climbs up again. Some birds stay for the summer, others pass through on the way to more northern nesting grounds. The song sparrow that nested at the end of Ashland Avenue the last two years is back. I see him in the same spot—same tree, same perch, same song; he drops low in a willow when I walk closer. The killdeers I hear every morning will nest only two hundred metres from my home, in the gardens between the river-bottom forest and the hospital.

Sometimes I lie down on the deck in my backyard in summer, evening, I close my eyes, I hear gulls calling, ring-billed and Franklin's, occasional Bonaparte's, they circle the sky far above me. Evenings like that my head fills with the sound of gulls, sound of quiet and gulls, I dream that I live near the ocean; St. John's, San Francisco. Manitoba is a maritime province, we forget that, Churchill a saltwater port. But that body of salt water lies more than a thousand kilometres from Winnipeg, not exactly the reason those gulls sojourn here. The chief attraction for them probably the Brady Road landfill, lots of good food there; gulls have their jobs to do too, cleaning up human waste. It might be a tainted allusion, some people hate gulls, something dirty about them, their scavenging. But I love to just lie back and listen, as the sun falls, the gulls high in the sky, and calling. A beautiful call. I close my eyes. On evenings like that my head floods with the sound of gulls, the sound of quiet and gulls and waves. Evenings like that I dream of a shack on the beach by the ocean.

*Bank swallow (left) and
barn swallow (right)*

Springtime and Calving

*I*ce. Glacial ice. Hard to believe that sixteen thousand years ago Manitoba lay buried beneath several kilometres of ice. Sixteen thousand years. Not that long when you think that the human species have been around for more than a million, if you think of the big brontosaurs wandering the plains almost 200 million years ago, when you read about the earth's apparent four-billion-year history. Most of the landscape we see driving today in Manitoba was shaped by the retreat of that last recent glaciation. Hills and valleys, end-moraines and sand pits and eskers, flats and coulees. The gentle Pembina River near Windygates—more like a creek now—must once have filled that Pembina valley, three kilometres wide, raging spring torrent carrying glacial melt-water east and south, perhaps for thousands of years. Glacial ice, imagine, two kilometres thick, so that the earth's surface bent and sagged with the weight. The Wisconsinan. You wonder where all that ice could have come from. What could have caused that last ice age, why did the earth's climate cool and allow such an onslaught? Was it a change in the output of heat from the sun, in the composition of the atmosphere? Was it a shift in the earth's orbit, in the position or height of the continents, a revision in the movement and swirl of the oceans? Scientists believe a mean annual drop in temperature of as little as six degrees Celcius would have created the necessary conditions. Doesn't sound like much. Climatologists, last night on the television, predicted that our Canadian summer this year would reach four degrees above the average; what effect might that have on our planet?

North and east out of Winnipeg. Main Street, Disraeli Bridge, Henderson Highway, the Perimeter. Winding through traffic, morning traffic, people with their ordinary lives, their ordinary routes to their ordinary jobs. North on Lagimodiere Boulevard, Highway 59. No ice here. Except inside me. Cold. Numb. My hands tremble on the steering wheel, my Honda speeds and slows, bumps on the right edge of the pavement. I'm not doing well, I've lost the pleasure of this game, this Oak Hammock game I started three years ago, I need to concentrate. I wish my life could feel ordinary again.

Past the floodway and the town of Birds Hill. Past Garven Road, Coronation Road. The park, Birds Hill Park, that ridge of gravel and sand dumped by the Wisconsinan Glacier, waiting now in the morning sun. Communities of trembling aspen, bur oak, balsam poplar, white spruce; stands of eastern white cedar, black spruce and tamarack. Astonishing information: aspens, though they produce seed, spread primarily by cloning. Parent trees send up shoots or suckers that grow into more parent trees, one forest of aspen may have cloned from as few as two or three different source trees, trees from one clone will all leaf or change colour at the same time. I've picked up a list of the wildflowers growing in the park throughout the growing season, more than 250 species of flowering plants, I've studied them in my wildflower book. Early blue violet, hoary puccoon, three-flowered avens, golden Alexander. Wild columbine, yellow lady's slipper, thimble weed. Pussytoes, purple milk vetch, giant hyssop, prairie lily, northern bedstraw. Wild bergamot, blue-eyed grass. Beyond the park, black-and-yellow signs, *Deer Crossing*. And a deer carcass splayed on the paved shoulder, roadkill, crows gathering all around it. I notice that the wheat fields of southern Manitoba have suddenly disappeared, the highway bound by meadow and grass and parkland.

Beyond Lockport, East Selkirk. Past Cook's Creek and Dubas Creek, Devil's Creek. Beyond the sturdy wire fence and a herd of grazing bison, or are they beefalo? After the grain elevator at Libau, I turn east on the 317 toward Lac du Bonnet. A cluster of tree swallows dawdles here at the intersection. I watch them for a second in my rearview mirror, glimpse a warning behind them in the west, the sky black and stormy. I pass farmyards and starlings, fences, a herd of cattle, a couple of pale spring calves in the pasture. A few grain fields here, curved and skirting the poplars. There, a red-winged blackbird, ruffled feathers, he's bucking the wind. I pass a small graveyard, Libau East Cemetery. I wonder about the people that might be buried there. What nationalities? Nepinak, Hamilton, Lysack, Woelcke? I remember from some of my outings that Native Canadians still live in this area. Tommy Prince, the decorated World War II hero, was born in the Brokenhead Ojibwa Nation nearby. As well as Métis. I once went fishing with a couple of guys who lived here, friends of a friend, I've forgotten their names. British settlers, of course, came to build their homes near the posts of the Hudson's Bay Company; the Polish and Ukrainian, Scandinavian immigrants arrived late in the nineteenth century, and Icelandic. The word *Libau*, according to my encyclopedia, suggests Latvian or German origins, a group of German Lutherans raised their first church on the site opposite the current east gate of Birds Hill Provincial Park.

On my right a sign for the Libau Bog Ecological Reserve. I was surprised several years ago to hear about the Libau

Bog, its canopy of black spruce and tamarack, its juniper and red osier dogwood and dwarf birch. An old and poorly drained lake, a thick rug of live and rotting organic matter floating on the water. Libau Bog, five hundred acres of reserve where as many as eleven species of orchid grow. Round-leaved bog-orchid, dragon's mouth, grass pink, ram's head lady's slipper, green adder's mouth, showy lady's slipper, leafy white bog-orchid, small northern bog-orchid. Some, the sparkling dragon's mouth, rare and endangered; others, of the bog-orchid species, quite unadorned in appearance. Like many of the native wildflowers, all these plants so vulnerable to human activity.

Miles of conifer forest here along the road, white spruce, balsam fir, I stop the car to study bark and branches. And farther along more trembling aspen, long pale trunks, black knots and whorls. I pass hayfields; and farmers out with their tractors and harrows, their seed drills, their trucks and seed grain—here's a male kestrel hunting. I cross the Brokenhead River. Drive under a large flock of gulls, black hoods, red bills, Franklin's gulls. Pass a mourning dove on a wire, a western meadowlark singing, old and broken buildings, deserted barnyards. More black spruce, their crow's-nest tops; and tamarack, deciduous conifers, growing their supply of this year's needles. A patch of whitetop along the side of the road. I notice a rise in the highway ahead of me, end-moraine ridge—it extends all the way from Victoria Beach south and east through Sandilands Provincial Forest to the Minnesota border—where the glacier paused in its slow retreat to dump large amounts of debris off its outer edge.

This is the country, fifteen months ago, where Susan and I drove on a Sunday morning in February looking for owls. Highway 317 and Maple Creek Road. One owl on any given day should be enough excitement for anyone, polished birder or city slicker, but we found forty-two owls that Sunday. Owls perched in trees, on fence posts and electric posts. Owls hovering. Owls hunting. Owls resting. Owls flapping and stooping for prey, flying low over long white fields, sometimes three owls within a hundred metres of each other. Forty-two owls; twenty-two of them great grey owls—a species Susan had never seen before—seventeen northern hawk owls, two snowy owls; they hardly noticed us watching from a dozen metres away. White fields. Lots of snow that year. Maybe the rodent populations had fallen in other parts of Manitoba and Northern Ontario, maybe the snow was just too deep for easy hunting. Those owls had gathered *here* in an effort to survive the winter, hoping to stay alive through the winter. When we made that trip the following February we couldn't find one owl on the exact same route, we began to understand how unpredictable life could be.

Staying alive. So far this month Susan and I have thought a lot about the business of staying alive. What it takes, how to do it, we'd hoped for some easy answers. Numb! Numb! The doctors say that some of Susan's left side, after her mastectomy, will always stay numb, she will never regain all the feeling in her arm and her chest. Cancer, last week Susan was diagnosed with breast cancer. When you hear that word, *cancer*, ugly word, the bottom drops out of your universe, a bundle of fear parks on your doorstep, you already begin to think about the funeral. Susan just celebrated thirty-five, she doesn't want to die, hasn't lived nearly long enough. And it all happened so quickly. One day she was well, she was working, we talked at supper about being lucky, we started to plan the next vacation. Life felt normal, a bit boring maybe, I sat in the living room in the evening and wished for a little excitement. The next day Susan found a lump in her left breast. A tumour, 2.5 centimetres across, the doctor said the lymph nodes were involved. All those years the cells in her body worked together as a team, suddenly they're working against her, we're not so sure now we can trust the process of our lives. Happens so quickly. One doctor's appointment. One mammogram. A second doctor's appointment. Bone scan. Chest x-ray. Blood tests. A meeting with the oncologist. Two meetings with the surgeon. Before the half-month is gone, I wait on the ward for Susan to come out of surgery, I wish my life would turn boring again.

Susan on the gurney when she finally comes up to her room, so small, curled up, helpless, only half conscious. What can I do? I stand in the middle of the hospital hall and sob and sob. Maybe I'm not supposed to cry that way in front of all the patients, in front of Susan, she might think there's no hope left at all; nurses take me by the arm and lead me to the staff room, they put a cold cloth on my forehead, they pour ice water for me to drink. I hear them whispering among themselves. "He's still in shock," they say. They turn to me. "You have to be strong for her," they say. I can't imagine anymore what strength is.

These are the new words for our vocabulary, Susan's and mine. Mastectomy. Lumpectomy. Metastasize. Tamoxifen. Mammography. Reconstruction, recurrence. Prosthesis. Axillary dissection. Lymphedema. Sarcoma. As if by naming them I can squeeze them in my hand, shape them. Ovarian oblation. Brachytherapy. Estrogen receptor. Benadryl. Cyclophosphamide. Epirubicin. 5-fluorouracil. Some words you wish you never had to learn, you wish your ears could turn them off. Where did this all begin? Was it when I turned forty, forty-five? Heart attack, aneurysm, and ambulance, a couple of friends in the hospital; I began to notice people dying around me. Maybe I woke one day, walked out in the garden, noticed in the heart of a red flower, *Lychnis chalcedonica*, that life was a certain kind of gift, each day a special kind of gift. It's surprising how quickly feelings can fall from joy to melancholy, rise again from despair to joy; we've talked about that, Susan and I, we've both noticed that, some days we still find moments of delight, the moon shining on our bed in the middle of the night.

Seven Sisters, Whitemouth, Pine Falls, Fort Alexander, Pinawa, Silver Falls, Great Falls; I enjoy these words, place names, their rhythms, the pictures they conjure. I see them strung out on the map, I tickle their syllables over my tongue, maybe they'll displace those others. At Highway 11 and Lac du Bonnet I turn north again. The road winds along the Winnipeg River—Cree, *win-nipi*, "murky river"— between outcroppings of pink rock, slopes back onto the flats, standing water in the ditches, a ring-necked duck pair, a female common merganser. Seven kilometres and I turn onto a driveway. Berent's place, a small ranch, cow-calf operation, Berent and I went to high school together in Ontario; I've been planning this outing for months. May, the wildflowers have started to bloom, right here in the grass beside me clusters of brilliant yellow flowers. Broad, almost geranium-like leaves, long quarter-inch green stems, five or six sepals on every cupped flower. Must be a yellow marshmarigold. My book says that all the parts of the fresh plant are poisonous—the leaves can even cause your skin to blister, though boiled or dried they become harmless. And twenty metres farther along, white cinquefoil, large pinnately compound leaves on a hairy stem, a flower with five white petals and a yellow centre. Cinquefoil roots were used in the past to produce dyes and to tan leather; *Potentilla*, the Latin name, refers to the effectiveness of these plants in stopping bleeding and dysentery.

Berent always wanted to be a cowboy, a rancher, even as a teenager, even his noon hours at school he loved to talk about rodeos and cattle. Now, after all those other jobs, he finally has his ranch, his 2,200 acres. Barns, and sheds, and bunkhouse. Charolais, Red Angus, Hereford. Truck and tractor. The barnyard swarms with birds: barn swallows, cliff swallows, house sparrows, tree swallows far above. Killdeers call, and robins, western meadowlarks, savannah sparrows. A downy woodpecker hammers and whinnies in the branches of a dead spruce, a white-crowned sparrow flits from the weeds. Somewhere north of the barn a song sparrow, I hear him; and an eastern phoebe perched and bobbing its tail on that blue metal gate, a pair of phoebes; a chipping sparrow lights on a patch of bare earth. Kestrel on a hydro wire; a warble of song, purple finch, in that open snag in the aspen. Ravens fly in the distance, an eastern bluebird above the pasture. Wren, American goldfinch, least flycatcher, white-throated sparrow, the winnow of a common snipe. Sandhill cranes circle over the treetops, twenty-two of them, same number as those great grey owls of Susan's. Golden quiet here, apart from the birds, the wind gathers and falls.

I wander back through the yard, past the paddock of bulls—Diamond S, that big, mean-looking Charolais—into the pastures north of the barn. Pitted and dried cow prints, splashes of dung on the rock, northern flicker male flies above me, yellow-shafted, his black moustachial stripe. More mounds of that pink rock here, granite, Canadian Shield, more than a billion years old, straight lines scratched across it, I can read the scour of the glacier as it ground first south and then north again. And lichens on that granite too, orange, pale green and blue; I think elegant orange lichen, this one, I kneel for a closer look. A mallard squawks from an acre of water and cattail. *Yip*, one single bark, must have been for the mallard; Pep, the farm dog, has caught up with me. Small dog, runt of the litter according to Berent, black, white and tan, Australian cattle dog, red heeler; company for me. I walk the fence line, echo the hum of the electric wire, trail beyond the pasture and into the bush. Aspen, white spruce, and more granite. Common goldeneye, green-winged teal in a pond. I follow the song of a ruby-crowned kinglet into a cluster of balsam fir. Evergreen, a perfect pyramid, Christmas tree, flat needles in two rows along each twig, balsam fir, the smooth grey bark with its resin blisters so much like the cherry trees back home. I walk past a chorus of frogs, boreal chorus frogs, past a tall thin birch, peeling bark, and a flutter of black-capped chickadees, follow the truck ruts toward a clearing in the forest I know Berent likes to harvest for hay. A giant anthill here, three feet in diameter, and mounded two feet high above the ground, one-centimetre-long black ants. No mosquitoes, but

Black-billed magpie

hundreds of ants, and I need to remember when I get home to check for ticks, Susan needs to be careful about insect bites since her surgery.

Spring, in the forest, on the farm. New birth. And suddenly all my interest, and drive, my curiosity for the world collapse around me. A quiet place in the bush for thoughts. For fear, doubt, some hours those just swallow you whole, nine out of ten nestling birds will not survive their first winter. I sit down on a rock and wait. I think about the weeks ahead of us. What happens now? What else will we need to do? What will the pathology show? What other agonies are left to be discovered? The jumble of emotions, anger, resentment, I just can't stand it, my hands begin to shake again. I think about loss, and mourning, Susan's, mine; I wonder about a time where each day again will be its own. The books say that cancer can be taken in stride, many people survive to find rich and happy lives, we should focus on learning, on healing and growth, attitude is every-thing they say, almost everything, we should surround our-selves with love. My sister, my sister-in-law, both of them have survived breast cancer, they call often. I look up at the sky, down at my hands, at Pep who looks back. Gentle rain has begun to wash over us, spring rain, harder now, within minutes I'm soaked to my skin; the sky, the storm from this morning's swallow corner has caught up with me, looks like it could rain all day.

Berent has built an art out of fencing. Wyoming fence, New Zealand fence, Kentucky, PFRA, and Haythorne gates; posts and rails and wire. He points them out to me; there, and there, marks their features, a bit of history. I asked him over the phone, he said 152 cows to calve this year, that's a lot of calves, it's the calves I've wanted to see. In the west pasture, after the rain has stopped again, I climb up onto a large bank of rock. Look at those calves. Ten, twenty, thirty, must be at least sixty of them. Calves everywhere, those stunning calves, those splendid calves. Beautiful tans. And reddish browns. Some of them ivory white. A few miniature Herefords. I walk out among them, among the calves and cattle. Caught between curiosity and fear, they start away from me, they turn around, watch, step a little closer, they start away again. Brown-headed cowbirds fly among them. The wonder of calves is that they're born, that they lie on the ground all wet and slippery, that their mothers lick them, that they dry. That they get up on their wobbly legs, they learn to walk. That they suck, they'll suck on your fingers if they get a chance, coarse tongue tickle on your fingers. That they don't get sick out there in the pasture, in the cold, after the rain falling. *Co-o boss, co-o boss*, I'm surprised that Berent still uses the same call for his cattle that my father used forty years ago in Ontario, where did they find that common language?

Here in the south corner of this pasture birds sing again, marking territory, their mating calls; bobolink, clay-coloured sparrow, common yellowthroat, northern oriole, and a sora. Eastern kingbirds, I've heard them for an hour or more, now I finally see a pair in that rusty tree. American toad calls from a nearby pond, its long melodious trill, a tape of Manitoba frog sounds arrived in my mailbox a few weeks ago. Great blue heron flaps overhead. The cattle continue to move, toward and away from me, they open a view to a solitary aspen, a Charolais mother beside it with two newborn calves, twins. One of the calves already dry, struggling to stand, the other still covered in mucus and membrane, the mother half-turned and eating the afterbirth. Three turkey vultures hunker on fence posts nearby, they would hope for a difficult birth, for a dead calf. Now the mosquitoes have caught up with me, droves of them, I pull the bottle of bug lotion from my back pocket, spread cream on my arms and neck.

When I get back to the yard, Berent and his hired man, Clint, have already begun work on the new fence, Berent with the saw, Clint beside the tractor and a load of rails. They call hello when they see me. I walk over, bend to gather hammer and nails out of a bucket, and join them. This kind of work, today, swinging a hammer, good for me, especially with friends, feels good to me, all of me, I feel good to be hammering nails. Later we'll sit down, the three of us, and eat lunch.

First the ground cloth. The hatchet and pegs. Poles, top fly, ropes. My nylon tent takes far longer to set up than I'd expected; a short memory, I've only used the tent four times in the decade. Almost sundown. I didn't want to start too early, some diligent Oak Hammock Marsh staff might catch me, I'm not sure this would be allowed, tenting, one of my Oak Hammock friends suggested that it was far better not to ask. I straighten from my task to watch mallards, green- and blue-winged teal, redheads float near the water's edge; watch that Canada goose pair waddle across the gravel with its clutch of goslings. Franklin's gulls curl overhead, and tree swallows, a black-crowned night heron flies. Brewer's black-birds, gadwalls, yellow-headed blackbirds, coots, lesser scaups. And muskrats. Savannah sparrow sings; killdeer call pierces the sky; farmer, seed drill and tractor again drone in the distance. I notice how the setting sun shadows the bright grass, I'd better get back to my work.

The marsh sun disappears at nine o'clock. No clouds in the western sky, the east shows a few. At nine-thirty I hear the first coyote call; and another coyote answer. Frog, toad, some insect in the pond behind me seems suddenly to *crick* much louder. I sit in my lawn chair and watch the darkness fall, now that the tent's done I can concentrate. So many birds migrate at night—ducks, geese, shorebirds, grebes, you can spot them with a scope against the moon—in the morning they settle into the marsh to rest and feed. Nighttime comes slowly in Manitoba, even after the sun has gone. Light still holds, and holds, waits and holds, some-times in summer the sky still bright even at ten-thirty. A few mosquitoes find me here, I brush them away. Shovellers still float by, and ring-necked ducks, that male holds his head so high. The marsh rattles and gulps, hums and buzzes and clacks, whinnies, snuffs. Sora, American bittern, some of those sounds. Far to the south I see the city begin to glow, I think of Susan settling to sleep at her parents' house, I didn't want to leave her alone so soon after surgery. Sometimes, lately, in the city I've noticed couples quarrelling, I watch how they treat each other, unkind, not that unusual. They've forgotten that they loved each other, why they lived together, forgotten that first touch, discovery, those early conversations. These days, Susan and I have found a new edge to live on, our communications have become clear, we talk, we listen, we hope to find that extra hour's pleasure.

I've pitched my tent on a patch of fresh alfalfa just to the west of the Oak Hammock Marsh north hill. An hour's work, good work, alfalfa a good choice, such a cushioned delight, I've taken a turn in the tent to retrieve my air mattress so I can blow it up outside. Even an hour after sunset, ten o'clock, the northern shoveller still bobs his head for his mate, marsh wrens still call, the Canada geese still wander with their young, the coyotes sing again, they can remember their love.

The things I've taken for granted: the years to come, the marsh, the pleasure of company. Stars, my dictionary still defines them as celestial bodies, then goes on to talk about gas and gravity and nuclear reactions. Now those stars begin to sprinkle the sky far above me. And planets. Venus, near the west horizon. Lyra, the harp. Orion, the hunter. Cassiopeia. Ursa Minor. Is that Mars, high in the east, its reddish glow? The sky bright with stars. The North Star, Polaris, see how it leads Ursa Major into the night. The light from Polaris, I've heard, has travelled since the death of Galileo Galilei, 1642, to find me here, today; I've brought a half-bottle of wine and a loaf of French bread to celebrate its 350 years. That probably isn't allowed here at the marsh either, the bottle of wine. At eleven o'clock, I hear a cow bellowing over in the pasture.

The marsh settles into night. I crawl into the tent with my mattress, lay out my sleeping bag, the pillow. I listen to the burr of insects outside, the breeze playing at the canvas, calming sounds, nighttime is when I fear the future most. Sometimes I'm surprised at Susan, how strong she is, how determined to live, to beat this disease. I see the joy she feels resting in the backyard in the sun after her surgery, when her parents come to visit, when her niece and nephew gather round. Sometimes I'm surprised how much joy we still experience. One of my sisters lives in New York state, she called a few days ago to tell us that the Society of Friends group she meets with had asked her to relay this message, that they are "holding Susan in the light." Morning, sunrise, warmth, still potent symbols for me, bringing plants and growth. The image suits my instinct, I imagine Susan now wrapped and comforted in a shining white ball. Even here, near midnight with darkness fallen, the white objects in my tent—my cooler, the label on the bottle of wine, my sport socks—carry a memory of that light. I ready myself for sleep. I'll leave that tent flap open in case a coyote comes to visit, maybe I'll wake and see it, just the screen closed against mosquitoes. I lie down, close my eyes, Susan in the circle of light . . .

Dick dick kidick kidick, dick kidick kidick kidick. That sound again and again, doesn't stop. *Dick dick kidick kidick.* The thought comes to me in my half-sleep, that's one of the rails out there, Virginia rail, like the sora, one of the marsh birds you seldom get to see. I pick up my watch, one-thirty, I move toward the screen. And gulls too calling, far away, must be a hundred or more. I hear the marsh wren. The stars even brighter now, sky splashed with stars. This time I close the tent flap, try to trap what little heat I might create, keep it inside. Fear of flying, fear of water, fear of heights, fear of enclosed spaces. Fear of the future, dreams and plans about to wipe off the slate. Fear of cancer. The trouble with cancer, you never know if you've won or lost. Fear of death, all animals seem to have that. I don't know what's more difficult, facing my own fear, when it comes, or watching Susan's.

Soon after three in the morning the tent begins to shudder and shake, somehow the wind has found me. A half-moon has risen, waning, but I'm far too tired to set up the scope now and look for migrants. I remember a story I read about someone who hiked out to camp in the New Mexico mountains; in the morning he found that a cougar had stopped beside his campfire in the night. I sleep again. My sleep is fitful, I dream of wolves and other attackers, one man is easily overcome. I sleep, and wake, sleep. Five o'clock, six, six-thirty. Red-winged blackbirds begin to call, and grebes, coots. I pull on my pants, my socks and shoes, step from the tent. A pair of phalaropes settles on the water in front of me, they spin and feed. Dark stripe through the eye, white up the back of the neck, Wilson's, one of only three phalarope species in the world. Phalaropes have the so-called gender roles reversed. The female, more brightly coloured than the male, does the courting, several females may chase one male, the male incubates and raises the young; a shorebird for the millennium. Double-crested cormorants have flown in overnight, they skim the cattails; and pelicans, a dozen of them; one ruddy duck male, regimented and proud. Cowbirds fly, a circle of eight black terns, buffleheads out over the water, a Forster's tern, the bobolink's bubbling song in the pasture. The sun shines from behind a bank of cloud. In the west the sky black again, another storm rolling in.

Hummingbirds; 319 species worldwide, all of them in the Western Hemisphere. Susan and I have seen a few hummingbirds in Manitoba, all ruby-throated, the others never fly here. One at our old house on Ashburn Street, August 27, 1993; it flew over the fence and into our perennial garden, poked at a few bright flowers, disappeared again. Another, on that same date three years later in our yard in Riverview, this one lingered at a hummingbird feeder we'd long since given over to a Baltimore oriole pair. Maybe two dozen other Manitoba sightings. But last year in Arizona we watched them at our leisure. Blue-throated hummingbird, black-chinned hummingbird, magnificent hummingbird— it really was, so dark and shimmering, green throat and purple crown—around the George Walker House where we stayed in the Chiricahua Mountains. We rested in the hammocks on our veranda while they fed just a few feet away. We noticed their buzzing sounds, we heard from inside the house when they flew into the yard, we finally began to feel comfortable identifying them, even the less distinctive females. The blue-throated, largest of the North American hummers, was so aggressive, bullied all the others around.

Down the highway in Patagonia we wandered into a private backyard, all birders were welcome, sat down to watch a group of feeders, ten, twelve hummingbirds feeding at one time. Anna's, Costa's, violet-crowned, broad-tailed, even one rufous hummingbird, sometimes they flew within inches of our heads, we couldn't help but dodge. Their energy, their dazzling colours, their ability to hover, fly backwards, sideways, their speed; hummingbirds, because of their high metabolism, feed almost continually just to stay alive, they need to increase their body weight by half before migration. In Tucson another bird enthusiast led us to a bush, parted the branches and pointed at a delicate nest. What a sight! Broad-billed hummingbird nest; grass and leaves and bark. One egg the size of a white navy bean, and a nestling not much bigger, such a tiny bundle of hope.

Several raindrops catch me in the face, cool wash on my face. Wind, the storm, I'd better hurry. I don't bother to pack the tent, throw it in the trunk instead, cooler and sleeping bag, I'll clean them up at home. I stand for a while in the storm, slide into the car, sit and listen to the rain on the car roof, on the windshield. I start to think of rain as healing, the feel, and the sound of it, the smell. I love the sound of rain on metal, the drum and rhythm of rain on the roof of the car, I love the sound of rain, so soothing. I take a deep breath, fresh breath, down into my lungs, I'll have to take Susan out in the rain, I think that rain bestows healing.

Double-crested cormorant

From Pole to Pole

A tired-looking aircraft waits on the runway. Faded paint, old fuselage and wings, rough and ready, the look of a predator; we step across the tarmac and onto the stair. *Hawker*, after the builder, this aircraft, HS748 the more official signifier, though nothing about *this* machine looks official. The steward at the door tells us the seating is open, the seat numbers on our boarding passes apparently don't mean a thing. "Oh," he says, puzzled, as though he's never heard of assigned seating, the only seats left just over the wing. Torn fabric inside. Mismatched plastic panels and smudges of glue. Hole in the pane of one of our windows. The bathroom improvised, lots of duct tape to hold the pieces together. Only one consolation, the Rolls Royce insignia stamped on the housing of the engine, old-fashioned quality. The Canadian North is famous for its aviation, daring, and narrow escapes, and bush pilots; reminder of the days of real adventure, the days of Munk and Franklin and Hearne. I've read about them, their Arctic explorations; Henry Hudson cut adrift to the open sea by his crew in

1611; Sir John Franklin, I've traced his travels with my finger on a map. We feel like rookies here, Susan and I, everyone around us dressed in blue jean, top and bottom, the two of us in ironed cotton pants. Rookie, the first hour up I keep looking out my window to check the engine, make sure the propeller's still turning.

Six people, seven days, in a big old Ford van, windows all around, another woman besides Susan—I'm glad about that. We've come out looking for birds. We've studied our bird books, we've printed lists, lots of species we'd like to see here: Pacific loon, Ross's gull, whimbrel, red-necked phalarope, Smith's longspur, willow ptarmigan, sharp-tailed sparrow. We drive back and forth along the Coast Road. To Button Bay. To Bird Cove. Down Twin Lakes Road. Goose Creek Road, Eskimo Point, Scrap Metal Road, Landing Lake Road. Churchill, Manitoba, salt water and shipping, a lookout on the northern sea. Such a small town, so far from the prairie hub, and all that fog, permafrost just eighteen inches below the surface of the ground, easy to forget a place like that. But the residents of Churchill also live at the juncture of three biomes, three biological communities, Arctic tundra, boreal forest and Arctic marine; a great place to look for birds.

Churchill. Flat, and hills and rough. Churchill. Picture rock. Masses, and fields of rock, in jumbles, in piles and scattered. Grey rock, black rock, copper and golden-brown rock. Beaches of rock. Canadian Shield. And trees. Stunted spruce and willow, dwarf birch. Krummholz near the shore, those one-sided spruce trees trained by wind and flying ice particles. Farther inland, up Twin Lakes Road, white spruce, tamarack, black spruce, much like on the highway from Winnipeg to Lac du Bonnet. And dwarf mistletoe, the parasite that grows in clumps at the top of spruce trees—along with spruce budworm and fire, forestry, one of the significant forest enemies. Forty-seven species of willow, we're told, around Churchill. These willows often browsed by herbivores, moose, caribou or hare, species for whom they also provide bedding and cover. Native people once used the bitter willow bark to control pain and fever, salicylic acid.

Wildflowers, we take pictures, a cheap camera. White mountain-avens, bog buck-bean, Labrador tea. One of our group gives me lessons in wildflowers, she bends low to the ground. "Stemless raspberry, see the three leaflets, reddish-pink flower." Up again, and pointing. "Purple paintbrush, those long stems, red bracts and flowers. There, pink corydalis, sometimes called rock harlequin. See the flower? I used to call it the bubblegum plant. That? Long-stalked stitchwort." I begin to follow in her book. Northern and seaside buttercups, most buttercups have a poisonous burning sap. Large-flowered wintergreen, its white flowers, the plant can be boiled for a medicinal tea. Flame-coloured lousewort, and bog rosemary. Common butterwort, those delicate purple flowers, the sticky surface of the leaf traps mosquitoes and ants, midges, absorbs them. Northern hedysarum— sweet vetch, the local name—all along the road, whole meadows of purple flowering vetch, the smell crazy in our noses as we drive along the road. Greenland primrose, alpine arnica, northern goldenrod, fireweed. All these wildflowers. Speckled horsehair lichen hanging from the branches of conifers, waxpaper lichen on the bark, woolly coral on the forest floor. Elegant orange lichen and button lichen on the rocks at Cape Merry.

Miles of tundra, marsh, so many puddles and ponds, but not one red-winged blackbird; red-wings stop just short of coming this far north in Manitoba, though they do nest far into the Territories north of Alberta. Maybe it's the ice those red-wings don't like. Ice, still on the Hudson Bay, even in July. Floes, and small bergs, chunks and pans; shapes of dragons, Inuit sleds, ships and bears and crocodiles. White ice, and brown ice, aqua green and dirty grey. We sit on the rocks at Cape Merry and watch the ice, watch how the sun kindles and shadows the ice, how it drifts with the tide, crowds against rocks, passes first upstream into the Churchill River, turns again when the wind shifts. One black guillemot swims between the ice floes, swims and disappears, dives, a hundred metres north of us. We study the ice wall, that large barrier of ice and rock on the horizon, looks like it runs for miles and miles across the water; apparently it's a mirage. They say that's why so many islands used to appear on ancient maps of the Arctic region, sailors used to sketch that ice wall onto their charts.

Most things human here around Churchill look terribly out of place, lost against this wide and barren landscape. The town lies spattered among the rock and gravel. Hangars, warehouses, buildings of galvanized sheet metal, rusted iron piled in the forest, stakes and poles on the tundra, spent missiles nose down in arctic meadows. Government, army, industry; what impresses you most, all the junk they've left behind. And one exception, our view of the Prince of Wales' Fort from across the river at Cape Merry. Low, and flat to the ground, built of stone, born of stone, crafted to belong among all those mounds and humps and hummocks, all those other rock formations.

We sit on the rocks at Cape Merry and hope for the wind to change. We need a strong north wind, cooler weather, we need to get rid of the bugs. An average July temperature of twelve degrees Celsius, Churchill, at thirty degrees, has actually been the hot spot in Manitoba the last two days. We've heard that the Ross's gull we're looking for has probably gone out with the ice and the south wind. The Ross's gull, small gull, with its pale rose breast, its wedge tail and black collar, has traditionally nested in northeast Siberia—Soviet Union—where few people were allowed to see it. But since the early 1980s several pairs have found their way to Churchill. That first nest in 1980 was apparently stolen and sold, along with the eggs, to a British collector; the next year's nest was given a twenty-four-hour guard. Funny how the wind blows here at the cape. Warm wind. Suddenly a pocket of cold, we begin to shiver. Five minutes, then warm again. Odd the way the weather moves along the Hudson Bay. Thunderstorms seem to want to move around Churchill, south or north of town, rather than above, often they have blue sky on either side of them. These rocks at Cape Merry still rebounding from the weight of the Wisconsinan Glacier, rising one-half metre every hundred years; that recoil, geologists predict, should continue for another six hundred centuries.

Caribou, we see them on the tundra, and seals, along the shore, one silver fox skirting a pond. Beluga whales with their calves dip and roll, white humps and flukes, blowholes, spout and spray; we watch them swim in the mouth of the Churchill River. My breath catches every time I hear a beluga blow, breathe, sounds so close, tender, and full of love. The first time though, I admit, I thought maybe it was a polar bear yawning behind the rock I leaned on. We stop out on the river in a boat and the pilot lowers a microphone into the water while the whales squeal and sing around us. That sound, over the speaker, everyone on the boat begins to "Ooh" and smile. There was a polar bear here just yesterday, at the Churchill Northern Studies Centre. One of the researchers, out sunning herself in a lawn chair, stumbled for the door when a white bear stepped round the corner of one of the buildings. We've been warned about polar bears, this time of year they're coming off the ice and moving inland. Just like Anna, her year in India, far too dangerous, we shouldn't ever walk out alone. Even at night, as I fall asleep, I think of polar bears crashing through my bedroom door.

Mosquitoes. The first thing people tell you about when they hear you're going north. Mosquitoes, black flies, midges, bulldogs. What a horror! Hum and buzz and swarm. Even here in the wind at Cape Merry, Susan, beside me, standing in a cloud of mosquitoes, must be several hundred of them prowling on her hood. We're glad now that we brought our bug pants and jackets, though sometimes we wonder if the DEET will eat our skin. Still, these jackets can't keep the black flies out, they must have somehow crawled inside the sleeves, my arms beginning to bleed and swell. By the third day in Churchill the drone of insects so constant in my ears I hear them everywhere, slap at dream mosquitoes on my neck.

We stand, binoculars and scope, and watch the birds. Whimbrel flying over, wandering to feed on the rocks. Common eider lazy along the shore. White and surf and black scoters, in large flocks, diving for mollusks and lifting in long lines off the water. Bonaparte's gulls spin and dive. Parasitic jaeger. It waits, drifts above the waves. Suddenly its flight strengthens, somewhere an Arctic tern has caught a fish. The jaeger chases and deals, pivots and rolls, snatches the fish mid-air when the tern finally tires of their game. Pacific loon, thin straight bill and purple throat patch. Harlequin duck, chestnut sides and short white ribbons. Least sandpipers. Semipalmated sandpipers. Lesser yellowlegs scramble from their eggs. Hudsonian godwits fly, flash their banded tails, their ruddy breasts, scream and circle in alarm as we pass through the nesting tundra. The land rings with the call of birds, loud with the cry of birds, warnings and pleas, seductions.

We wait on the rocks, the six of us, or in the van, we squash bugs and scratch, we talk about birds. We tell bird stories, birdwatching stories. The year somebody here at Churchill found an osprey nest and a chick peering over the edge. The year they saw a peregrine on that hydro erector. The year the brown thrasher flew across the road in front of the van and into the brush, a rare thrasher in Churchill. The rough-legged hawk that nested on the ladder at the satellite launch pad. We talk of spectacular window hits. The ruffed grouse that crashed through someone's kitchen window south of Winnipeg, landed on the floor, and then flew right back out again. The sharp-shinned hawk that flew against a picture window after picking a chickadee off the backyard feeder. We talk about other birders. One year, for a joke, Charlie tacked the skin of a three-toed woodpecker to a tree in a burn east of Churchill so he could bring his birding friends to see it. "Shh, we don't want to scare it." About early birders; Eva Beckett, the Churchill naturalist who reported a Texas bird, scissor-tailed flycatcher, in the 1940s. We talk about other great bird locations: Arizona, Maine, Florida, Galapagos, Peru. We talk about the beauty of names, bog buck-bean, how the words run together. About language, how to pronounce scoter, gyrfalcon, plover, guillemot. We talk about the weather, how unusual this heat is, sometimes in July birders have worn their long underwear and their gloves and parkas.

Churchill. North. Sun. Land of the midnight sun. We've been so busy with birds I've hardly thought about the sun. When we first arrived I was upset that our bedroom didn't have a window, I complained to Susan, I like to wake up with the light at my bedroom window. With our bird hours though, five thirty a.m. until midnight, I'm fighting exhaustion. Of course, we're not nearly far enough north for the sun to shine through the night, but I'm glad now about the window. On our second-last night in the north I get up every hour, leave my room and walk downstairs to the nearest window, check the position of the sun. One o'clock in the morning, pale blue sky in the northwest, cold at night but still very buggy when I open the door. Three o'clock, sunrise, northeast. Two hours of dark, how would I ever have slept?

Real adventure. Jens Munk and Samuel Hearne. Is there any of that left? Exploration. I'm sure the astronauts and cosmonauts would say so—journeys to outer space. And people who climb Mount Everest. The man who lost his fingers and toes kayaking the Arctic, frostbite. Is that adventure, or merely trivial? How do we judge adventure? By the risk? The possibility of death? In that case, Susan and I have found adventure too. Churchill, that was two years ago, two years before cancer. I've read that the Chinese character for crisis links two distinct words, danger and opportunity. The right mix of excitement and dread.

Beautiful morning. Just after the solstice. The first time in weeks that we've wakened to clear sky, a very wet June.

Trans-Canada Highway. Grey Volvo wagon, roof racks, paddles and canoe, driving east out of Winnipeg. The rising sun casts a shimmer across the prairie, as of a world scarcely born. Buildings, trees glisten and glow. We talk about that, Daryl and I, our hazy world. Reminder of yesterday's rain? Threat of pollution? "Reminds me of India," I say, "driving in New Delhi in the early morning before the day's heat catches you." And so we talk about India; jumble voices, house crows, dung fires lit by the ricksha drivers on street corners to take the chill off the dawn. We talk about Churchill, Daryl's been there too, taken a canoe trip on the Seal River north and west of Churchill. Much more familiar with the natural world than I, with rivers and bush, he's canoed large parts of this province, they seem like large parts to me, goes out for weeks on his own.

Moss Lake. Bare Hill Lake. Just across the border in Ontario, western fringe of Lake of the Woods, Daryl's old country. He used to go there often, day or weekend outings with his canoe, no roaring boats, no water skis to harass him. Until four years ago. Used to put up a winter camp, tent in the forest, firewood and tin stove, he could walk across the lakes in the afternoon and spend a winter week. Before they clear-cut the portage, a thousand acres either side, mixed pine and spruce, left a naked trail and naked strip of land between the lakes. Daryl and I have seen a lot together, marriage and work and kids, twenty years, he's agreed to take me there, to the lake country, we'll spend the day together.

Wild roses grow in the ditch and beside the train track here thirty minutes east of the city. Prickly rose, by the book, its thorns and bristles, far more prevalent in Western Canada than the common wild rose. Most parts of the native rose shrubs are edible, three rosehips apparently contain as much vitamin C as an orange. Rosehips may be boiled for tea or jam, or fermented to make wine. Native people once boiled the lower stems and roots to make eye drops to cure snow-blindness, used the inner bark as tobacco. Daryl has boiled the leaves of common Labrador tea, a good drink, he went out two weeks ago to the bush and walked through large fields of it, picked a small bagful to take home. Clusters of small white flowers on a long stem, rust on the underside of oblong leaves; he's heard that people in the North use Labrador tea as an insect repellent, crush the leaves and rub them against their skin, he's anxious to try that.

Open prairie and grain drift toward aspen, forest that Daryl says he finds particularly inhospitable, dense with undergrowth, heavy in mosquito and wood tick and poison ivy. I drove out the other day at dusk to look for a pair of scarlet tanagers that a friend told me was nesting in a new development east of Steinbach, forest edge along one of the pie-shaped lots on a cul-de-sac. I don't know what I was thinking, that I'd be able to spot the bird from the window of my car where I'd parked against a curb, that I'd walk out across somebody's lawn? Found instead a rutted and wet dirt track, a trail into the aspen thicket, clouds of mosquitoes, had to tiptoe in my shorts and sandals through bunches of poison ivy. I'd seen only two scarlet tanagers in eight years of birding, I decided that a third was worth a week's itching, the flaming scarlet of the male

tanager always such a surprise. Those birds, some-
times I wonder if they
glow in the dark, so
bright, and yet so
difficult to see.
I found him
though, the
male,
five
metres
up, near
the trunk,
singing from
the branches of an

Tree swallow

old oak. Firebird, a good second name for this tanager; probably somebody's joke to call it a black-winged redbird. I must have been lucky with the poison ivy.

Daryl's curious about the scarlet tanager, he wants to know more. Our voices struggle against the noise of the highway, the sound of the car, wind in the canoe. We cross a bridge and the Brokenhead River. Daryl tells me about the trees on either side of the road, one of the reasons I wanted to come out here, so he could teach me about trees. Tamarack, a deciduous conifer, pale, and delicate needles. Black spruce, a tall and narrow tree, the lowest branches sometimes droop to the ground and take root, the highest, if the soil is low in nutrients, tend to form a crow's-nest. These, jack pines, one-inch-long needles in pairs, flat and almost twisted, not a very dense tree, not at all the typical triangular conifer shape. Mature jack pine cones may remain closed on the tree for many years until they're opened by fire or exposure from cutting, they pioneer the new forest. White spruce, stiff and pointed needles, trunks sometimes as big as two feet across.

We pass mallard families in puddles, white-tailed deer feeding, clusters of eastern white cedar on the forest rim. The landscape changes, begins to roll, rocks gather along the road, and turkey vultures. Red pine here, sparse needles as much as six inches long, large reddish-brown scales of bark. And white pine, what a pleasure to see, broad and irregular, sweeping branches, even in the crown, reminder of the paintings by Emily Carr and the Group of Seven. One horizontal row of branches added each year, white pine trunks were valued as ship masts in the seventeenth and eighteenth centuries.

Insects swarm as we step from the car, while we collect our sacks, disappear as suddenly once we're in the canoe, those first four strokes of the paddle. Lake, all around us, and trees on the other side. Our paddles in the water, swirl at the end of a stroke, drip and splash. Dark water, black green water if you look straight down. And glassy smooth ahead. "Brackish," Daryl says, "and rusty when you see it in a pot." My arms and shoulders, my waist, rowing, an unfamiliar motion. Am I doing this right? With Daryl straight behind me, the thousands of miles he paddles, I don't want to lose a friend over a few faulty movements.

"Three bays here on Moss Lake," he says, "we'll paddle around them, close to the shore." White-throated sparrows call, and ruby-crowned kinglets. Song sparrows, a red-eyed vireo, robins, Swainson's thrush, though we don't see any of them. A jumble of calls sometimes, four birds at once, I point, try to separate the calls for Daryl. A pair of loons rises in the lake to our left, Canada jay on a branch to our right, two bald eagles above. More eastern white cedar along the water's edge. Balsam fir, jack pine, I rehearse the features of trees, best to practise while I have someone around to correct me. Irises growing here along the shore, blue flag the common name, lots of them, standing right in the water. And bright yellow flowers, two inches across, poked above their clusters of floating leaves, small yellow pond-lily. Now several species of wood warbler begin to sing all along the shore. The quiet of this landscape, the music of the forest and lake, our voices, oars, a few birds, no other sound.

A layer of cloud, light sun nudging through, I stop paddling and study the shoreline. Trunks of dead trees angle over the water. Patches of rock, white lines streaked across them, water levels. Moss and lichen growing. That shrub everywhere along the bank, slender and brown branches, lance-shaped leaf with a toothed and rounded tip, fragrant leaf when I break one, flowers in yellow-green catkins. Looks like sweet gale, a plant that can change sex from year to year, may grow male flowers one year, female the next. Green alder behind the sweet gale, elm-like leaves, reddish bark. Alders so important to northern ecosystems, they flower early, bees use alder pollen to raise their first broods, ruffed grouse eat the new leaves and buds. A chipping sparrow there in a white birch. Dragonflies over the water, and horseflies. Shamble of branches and mud, beaver lodge at the mouth of a creek. Suddenly an osprey splashes hard onto the back of a fish.

Daryl steers the canoe toward an outcropping of rock on the west shore, we're stopping for tea. Bucksaw and short-handled axe. The sound of that axe, it rings every time it strikes the wood. A thin axe with a broader head than the one I have at home; Daryl says it's Scandinavian, specially tempered steel. The fire takes just a few minutes to build, the tea leaves longer to brew. What do men talk about when they're out in the bush, when they sit in the smoke of a small fire sipping mint tea? Do they talk about beer? About secretaries, and hunting? Neither Daryl nor I have ever hunted, we have no bucks or antlers to compare. Instead, we trade stories about common whippoorwills, how they've kept us awake at night camping. We talk about family; our parents, how difficult they can be, or how appealing. We talk about our children—though they're almost too old for the word—the splendid things they do. Smell of the camp-fire, ripple on the water, wind brushing over us as we crouch on the rock. A wood tick crawls on my sleeve. The clouds darker now. Daryl asks about Susan, about her cancer. "How's she doing?" So we talk about that.

"No, she's not," I say, "Susan isn't working. She's taken a leave from her job, she says she wants to concentrate on being well. She's gone for physio, after the surgery her arm seemed almost frozen to her side. She exercises. They call it a radical modified mastectomy. An aggressive cancer so the chemotherapy will be aggressive too." I tell Daryl all I know about cancer, all I've learned, mainly from Susan, she's read a lot. About the stages of development; stage one, stage two, three. About the treatment; chemotherapy, six months, a twenty-eight-day cycle. And radiation afterwards. About bone scans and liver scans, about the MRI coming up next week.

Pink corydalis blooms beside me, I lean and touch it to my nose. Yellow-bellied sapsucker clatters in a jack pine. An ovenbird calls, strident. One common loon spins closer and closer, anxious to get a look at us. "So far, the chemo's not too bad," I say, "the side effects, she hasn't been sick, she rests a lot. Fourteen days of drugs, fourteen days' rest. She's gone out and bought a bunch of hats and scarves though, because of her hair. Colourful, she looks really good with a scarf tied on her head," I say.

"But do you know anything? Do you know what it means?" Daryl says. "Not really," I say. "We just try to make every day a good one, that's been working. I guess you and I could up and die tomorrow, couldn't we?" I say. We're quiet for a while and then Daryl talks about volcanoes and spiders. Spiders, he says, when they migrate, climb high in a tree. They let out a thread that might carry them for hundreds of miles on the wind, they're the very first creatures to return to a volcanic site. They live off the bacteria that grow on volcanic ash. A kind of miracle. Their excrement, and the excrement of other insects that follow, provides enough compost to support plants.

The portage to Bare Hill Lake carries us through the clear-cut—young aspen, wild strawberry, trillium, lots of ticks too—and high over a ridge. The north shore of the lake steep and rocky, trees cut to within forty metres of the water. Huge pines here, red pine and jack pine, white pine, some trunks four feet in diameter. The water levels look high this year, all along the lake's edge brown and drowned conifers. We paddle. Fast, to find the beaver dam as Daryl predicted. West, far to the other end of the lake and a large black-spruce bog. Shallow there, reeds, more blue flag. Round a point, at the base of a dead tree, suddenly a brown creeper flies. It whispers and scrambles up the trunk, disappears behind a patch of bark, creepers usually nest behind the bark of dead trees. We float for a while wedged among the deadfall, hoping to see the creeper again. We unpack our lunches: l'Envol cheese, garlic sausage and buns, oatmeal and apricot muffins, sliced English cucumber, apple. American tree sparrow calls and flies, short hops, alarmed at our presence. And a swamp sparrow, low beside the canoe.

Yellow-rumped warbler, Blackburnian warbler, a northern parula male feeding a fledgling. Together we name a few more plants. Knotted rush, its rusty brown heads; tufted loosestrife, yellow bottlebrush flowers.

A good day to be out, lots of cloud cover, we don't have to worry about heat or sunburn. We paddle east again, to an island where a bald eagle perches in a snag, it's waited there all afternoon. White pine island. There, through the foliage, fifty metres west of the perch, an eagle's nest. We beach the canoe and tie it to a shrub. Richardson's alumroot growing here, pale purple flowers on a foot-long leafless stem. And skunk currant, maybe. I rub one of the leaves, is that a strong enough smell? Rough cinquefoil, beside the canoe. After supper Daryl finds an orchid farther into the bush, he calls and I run to join him. Spotted coralroot, tiny flower. Look, the purple pinprick spots on its white lip. Early evening, our conversation has slowed by now, enough said, and my thoughts have drifted back to Susan.

I suppose Oak Hammock Marsh has changed in the last few years, not in the ways you might think, but that it's become more familiar, that I've become more comfortable here. That I remember how the marsh loosens on a pale blue morning in July, where the sun rises in the northeast, where the trails lead, their stages, I know how the heat will stifle when the temperature measures thirty-two degrees in the middle of the afternoon. The same Canada goose families wander round me where I walk. Yellow-headed blackbirds rasp again and call. Yellow warbler, clay-coloured sparrow, common yellowthroat sing, their early morning song, familiar song. American coot parents cackle on the water, gather their young. The first marsh wren rattles. Barn swallow and black tern weave the cool air, warp and weft.

The smell of marsh water. I stop. Something new, I'm not sure that I ever much smelled the marsh before. Acrid.

Sharp. Sewer smell, smell of rot. Stronger than other years I think, maybe because they've drawn down the water in one of the cells here to foster the increase of marsh grasses. A killdeer calls, runs from the shadow of the wild sweet-clover, begs me to follow. Yellow sweet-clover, the smell of that on my fingers where I crush a flower. A song sparrow on the nodding-thistle. Bush of purple flowers on a heavy four-foot stalk, alternate leaves, jagged and prickly. Lots of nodding-thistle here, the head's sweet perfume. And wavy-leaved thistle, gorgeous two-inch flower ball. Sow thistle, pigs eat that plant, those young leaves at the base would taste good in my salad, acres and acres of sow thistle gleaming in the morning sun. Alfalfa, raceme of small flowers, in patches of yellow and green and blue. Lush growth all along my trail, more than I've seen at Oak Hammock before, so much rain this year. A black-crowned night heron barks overhead, greater yellowlegs stands at the pond edge.

I walk again, brush through vegetation, heavy walking, almost like snow. A sora calls from the cattails. Two pelicans fly, their orange legs. A ruddy duck male in that direction too, stiff tail, rust-brown back, white cheeks and black cap, his sky-blue bill bobbing. July, and that ruddy duck's still looking for a mate. There, another ruddy male, and a female. Back among the reeds six ruddy duck young with their mother, they leave the nest within a day of hatching, know how to swim and dive immediately. One of the few ducks that breed in both North and South America; I wonder about these ruddy males. Why haven't they flown off to moult like other drakes, mallard and shoveller, why are they still mating? A mallard hen leads her seven young; vesper sparrow flies, white outer tail feathers.

That silver-green plant along my trail, small blue dragonflies swarming all around. Long stalk, ridged, lots of narrow and pointed leaves, tiny yellow florets, strong wild smell. Must be prairie sage. A cluster of narrow-leaved sunflowers behind the sage. And foxtail barley everywhere, its feathered tuft. Brome grass, looks a bit like oats. What I've called whitetop for the last few years my new plant book calls common reed grass, apparently it exudes a sap that can be eaten as candy. Yellow evening-primrose, these lemon-coloured flowers on a leafy stalk. Avocet. Orange neck and head, upturned bill, long legs, striking black-and-white plumage. Have I mentioned its beauty? One lone avocet flaps beside me, shrieks an alarm to the world. Or the marbled godwit, its cinnamon wings in the sunlight, a large shorebird. Hundreds of shorebirds feeding now on the mud flats: yellowlegs—both species—Wilson's phalaropes, ruddy turnstones, pectoral sandpipers, the godwit towers above them. The wind has turned into the northwest, flies in my face, makes shorebird identification difficult. One pair of spotted sandpipers too, still beautifully speckled, their stuttering flight, bob and teeter as they walk.

I made a special trip to Oak Hammock in May to look with other birders for a garganey that someone had spotted there. A common Eurasian teal nesting all across northern Europe and Asia, seldom reported in North America, we found it dabbling with other ducks, blue-winged teal, mallards, shovellers, gadwalls. A quiet evening, handshakes and hugs for those who'd never seen it. How did that garganey get here? Could it have flown with a flock of blue-winged teal from Alaska in fall, wintered in South America? Was it blown off course last month by heavy winds as it left the Philippines headed for Siberia? Will it ever see its kind again? Will it try to mate with other teal here in Canada, cinnamon or green-winged, with northern pintail? How does instinct carry ducks back to old nesting grounds? Instinct, is it individual or communal, does it require a flock?

Suddenly a Franklin's gull screams above me, the plumage not that clear, it must have already begun its moult. The gull dives and flies straight at me, so that I crouch. It circles and screams, circles, a waning quarter moon sharpens the sky beyond. It dives again. And again. So that I keep my eyes above, and to all sides, wary. Now it's joined by a mate. I must have somehow stumbled near a nest. The marsh has changed in the few years I've walked here. How many years, I've lost track of time, since the fall Jon and Anna spent in India. The marsh now holds memories of all my other walks, the birds I saw, the muskrats, bald eagles. The stories I remembered, and told, stories of family, and other places, stories of Susan, chronicles lodged here in rocks and corners and grass. Here's the halfway bench where I waited years ago, bench of the cross and the wing-stretched cormorant. The marsh has changed, the trail grown so heavy. Here a couple of goldfinches feed in the thistle, strong smell of thistle, smell of rotting stinking marsh and blooming flower. Three hours' march in the twenty-five-degree sun, stop, and start, still no hint of relief from the heat, no bush or tree where I can hide, only the grass and the wildflowers around me. Like all experiments, you can never know where you might end; the marsh gives, and the marsh takes away.

So many things to think about in the middle of the night. A long hot day in the wetlands. A Franklin's gull. Deadlines, the writing still left to do. Garden full of weeds. The lawn wants mowing. All the things that trouble me. I don't know how to pray. Whether to beg, or argue. Whether anger works, a raised fist. If I should try to cut a deal. Whether anyone listens. Susan, sleeping beside me, dim figure beside me. I lay my hand on her naked chest, fingers brush the red scar on her chest. I take a deep breath in, I imagine myself breathing into Susan. "Healing in," I say, I whisper. I breathe out. "Illness out the window." Breathe in . . . and out . . . slow breath . . . Again and again. If wishes were horses, Susan would get well again, would live her share of years beyond me, if I had the power in my hands. If I only had the power in my hands. Breathe. "Healing in. Illness out the window." Can heaven be any more beautiful than our earth? Our earth. Breathe . . . Heal . . . Power in my hand . . . Whisper . . . Anything more beautiful than our earth? Whisper . . . Until sleep finally catches me.

Least sandpiper

Bibliography

Angell, Tony. *Ravens, Crows, Magpies, and Jays.* Vancouver: Douglas & McIntyre, 1978.

Barwise, Joanne E. *Animal Tracks of Western Canada.* Edmonton: Lone Pine Publishing, 1989.

Boothroyd, Peter. "Whooping Crane Records for Manitoba, 1943-1979." *Blue Jay.* Regina, 1980.

Didiuk, Andrew. "Whooping Cranes in Manitoba." *Manitoba Nature* (1975).

Dillard, Annie. *Pilgrim at Tinker Creek.* New York: Harper's Magazine Press, 1974.

Ehrlich, Gretel. *The Solace of Open Spaces.* New York: Viking Press, 1985.

Eiseley, Loren. *The Invisible Pyramid.* New York: Charles Scribner's Sons, 1970.

———. *The Star Thrower.* New York: Times Books, 1978.

Griscom, Ludlow. *Audubon's Birds of America.* New York: The Macmillan Company, 1950.

Harrison, George H. "Black-capped Chickadees." *Bird Watcher's Digest* 15, no. 3. Marietta: Pardson Corporation, 1993.

Johnson, Derek; Linda Kershaw, Andy MacKinnon, and Jim Pojar. *Plants of the Western Boreal Forest and Aspen Parkland.* Edmonton: Lone Pine Publishing, 1995.

Johnson, Karen L. *Wildflowers of Churchill and the Hudson Bay Region.* Winnipeg: Manitoba Museum of Man and Nature, 1987.

Line, Les and Franklin Russell. *The Audubon Society Book of Wild Birds.* New York: Harry N. Abrams Inc., 1976.

Little, Elbert L. *National Audubon Society Field Guide to North American Trees.* New York: Albert A. Knopf, 1980.

Lopez, Barry Holstun. *Desert Notes.* Kansas City: Andrews and McMeel Inc., 1976.

Matthiessen, Peter. *The Snow Leopard.* New York: Viking Press, 1978.

———. *The Wind Birds.* New York: Viking Press, 1973.

Nebraska Game and Parks Commission. *Nebraska's Threatened and Endangered Species: Whooping Crane.* Lincoln, Nebr., 1994.

Norris, Kathleen. *Dakota: A Spiritual Geography.* New York: Ticknor & Fields, 1993.

Pasquier, Roger F. *Watching Birds: An Introduction to Ornithology.* Boston: Houghton Mifflin Company, 1980.

Prescott, G. W. *How to Know the Aquatic Plants.* Dubuque: Wm. C. Brown Company Publishers, 1969.

Recovery of Nationally Endangered Wildlife Committee. *National Recovery Plan for the Burrowing Owl.* Ottawa, 1995.

Robinson, Gail. *Raven The Trickster.* London: Chato & Windus, 1981.

Seton, Ernest Thompson. *Animal Heroes.* Toronto: Morang & Company, 1905.

———. *The Birds of Manitoba.* Washington: Smithsonian Institution, United States National Museum, 1891.

Stout, Gardner D. *The Shorebirds of North America.* New York: Viking Press, 1967.

Symons, R. D. *Hours and the Birds*. Toronto: University of Toronto Press, 1967.

Teller, James T. *Natural Heritage of Manitoba: Legacy of the Ice Age*. Winnipeg: Manitoba Museum of Man and Nature and *Manitoba Nature* magazine, 1984.

Terres, John K. *The Audubon Society Encyclopedia of North American Birds*. New York: Wings Books, 1995.

Uhmann, Tanys. "Developing a Habitat Suitability Index Model for the Burrowing Owl of Southern Manitoba." Draft proposal, 1996.

Vance, F. R., J. R. Jowsey, and J. S. McLean. *Wildflowers Across the Prairies*. Saskatoon: Western Producer Prairie Books, 1984.

Wrigley, Robert E. *Mammals in North America*. Winnipeg: Hyperion Press, 1986.

Other references used in the writing of these essays include:

Microsoft Encarta 96 Encyclopedia. Microsoft Corporation, 1993-95.

1997 Canadian Encyclopedia Plus. McClelland & Stewart Inc., 1996.

The Manitoba Conservation Data Centre. Files and Statistics.